Contents

TG

The Making of
the Church

J. G. DAVIES
M.A., D.D.

*Edward Cadbury Professor and Head of the Department of Theology,
University of Birmingham*

MOWBRAY
LONDON & OXFORD

Copyright © J. G. Davies, 1960

ISBN 0 264 66961 4

This edition published 1983 by
A. R. Mowbray & Co Ltd, Saint Thomas House,
Becket Street, Oxford, OX1 1SJ

First published in 1960 by Skeffington, Hutchinson
Group.

Printed offset in Great Britain

British Library Cataloguing in Publication Data

Preface

TO REPRINT EDITION

The history of the Early Church, in the sense of the record of the ascertainable facts, does not change very much as the decades pass, but Church history as the narration of the facts in order to reveal their interrelationship and their meaning does not rest immutable. Church history in this second sense arises out of a dialogue between the historian and the past events, and since his perspective and circumstances may alter so his interpretation will not remain always the same. In the case of this present work, which is a reprint of a book first published over twenty years ago, the author does not consider that there is much, if anything, that is yet in need of reinterpretation. He is happy therefore that it is being made available once again to those who want an introduction to the life and doings of Christians in the patristic era. The text remains virtually unaltered but the suggestions about books for further reading have been brought up to date — although even here it is perhaps surprising, in view of much further study of the period, that quite a number of the works previously listed must still be regarded as standard.

It simply remains for me to express my gratitude to Mowbray for reintroducing this book to the reading public.

J. G. DAVIES

Prologue

At nine o'clock in the morning, on the high day of a Jewish festival, in or about the year A.D. 30, some dozen or so men came lurching out of the door of a house in a Jerusalem side-street, babbling incoherently. To many in the crowd that soon gathered it seemed that the men were under the influence of drink, but their leader, a bluff fisherman from Galilee, soon scotched this explanation by pointing out, reasonably and intelligibly, that it was still too early in the day for them to have consumed any great quantity of alcohol. He then went on to give what he and his companions considered to be the true explanation of the experience which they had just shared in the upper room of the house, and as a consequence of which they had come rushing out into the street.

'This,' he said, 'is what was predicted by the prophet Joel:

> "And it shall be in the last days, saith God,
> I will pour forth of my Spirit upon all flesh:
> And your sons and your daughters shall prophesy,
> And your young men shall see visions,
> And your old men shall dream dreams:
> Yea and on my servants and on my handmaids in those days,
> Will I pour forth of my Spirit, and they shall prophesy." '

Peter—for that was the speaker's name—then asserted that this fulfilment of one of God's promises was the outcome

7

of the life, death, resurrection and exaltation of Jesus of Nazareth.

'Uplifted by God's right hand and receiving from the Father the long-promised Holy Spirit, he has poured on us what you see and hear.'

This Jesus was therefore none other than the long-awaited envoy of God, the Messiah or Christ, the Anointed One.

These words were not without their effect upon his hearers. Deeply disturbed, they asked what they should do and were told:

'Be baptized in the name of Jesus Christ for the remission of your sins, and you shall receive the gift of the Holy Spirit. For the promise is meant for you and your children, and for all whom the Lord God shall call to himself.'

According to the account in the Acts of the Apostles, nearly three thousand people accepted Peter's direction and were baptized. So took place the birthday of the Church.

If we are to understand something of the nature of this body which was later to bestride the five continents and to number among its members more men, women and children than those belonging to any other religious group known to man, we must take seriously Peter's affirmation that its appearance in history was no mere accident but the bringing to fruition of God's plan for the human race and the fulfilling of the divine promises. If we then ask where these promises are to be found, the answer is in the sacred writings of the Jews —in the Old Testament, as we now call it—to which we must turn if we would also know exactly what these promises were.

The Old Testament tells the story of God's dealings with an insignificant Middle-Eastern race known as the Hebrews, from the time when the twelve tribes into which they were divided were united to form a nation under a certain Moses.

This story is set against the background of the whole of human history by the opening chapters of the first book, Genesis, which recounts God's creation of heaven and earth and of man himself. Man, however, was not satisfied with his position of inferiority to God and so rebelled against his Maker. In consequence, self-separated from the true source of his being, he lived a divided existence, at odds with himself and with his fellows, so that soon 'every human being on earth had corrupted his life'. God's method of coping with this situation was not to wash his hands of his creatures but to choose one man, Abraham, out of all the fallen mass of mankind, whose descendants were to be taught to live in harmony once again with God and were in their turn to teach the other nations of the earth. It was these descendants that were delivered by God from bondage in Egypt, united to him in a covenant or agreement, led into the promised land and provided with a king as his representative. This king, who, like the Queen of England at her coronation, was anointed, was known in Hebrew as the Messiah and in Greek as the Christ, that is to say as the Anointed One.

The Israelites, however, sat lightly to their agreement with God, assuming all too readily that theirs was a position of privilege rather than of responsibility. Despite the warnings of the prophets, they did not persevere in the way of righteousness and so they were brought to the suffering of the Exile in Babylon. After their return, apart from a short-lived independence under the Maccabean house, they were occupied by a succession of foreign powers, from the Persians in the sixth century B.C. to the Romans in the latter half of the first. But hope did not die. The prophets and their successors, the apocalyptists, declared the divine promises; they asserted that God would eventually break the power of evil, that he would set up his kingdom or rule which would be exercised either directly or through his Messiah and that a new covenant would be established. So the Jews looked forward with eager expectation to the Day of the Lord when the barrier of sin between God and men would be broken down and God's Spirit would be poured out upon them.

When Peter quoted the prophecy of Joel and stated that it had been fulfilled, he was intimating that the hope of Israel was now in process of realization, that the assault on evil had begun, that man and God could once again be at one with each other, since God's Messiah had come in the person of Jesus of Nazareth. This was the good news or gospel—the news of promises honoured—with which the Church went forth into the world. Here, then, was no static body, as Israel of old, but a New Israel, dynamic, conscious of a mission to mankind, conscious of a presence with them which would enable them to execute their mission; conscious, in the words of one of the first missionaries, 'that neither death, nor life, nor angels, nor principalities, nor things present, nor things to come, nor powers, nor height, nor depth, nor any other creature, shall be able to separate us from the love of God, which is in Christ Jesus our Lord'. This conviction is scarcely intelligible except on the basis of the belief that 'Christ died for our sins according to the scriptures; and that he was buried; and that he hath been raised on the third day according to the scriptures'.

In essentials the message of the first missionaries by whose labours the Church was to grow was quite simple, consisting as it did in the proclamation that 'God was in Christ reconciling the world unto himself'. It was a message of salvation from sin and even from death, of hope in suffering, of courage in fear and of love uniting God with man and man with man in a fellowship which transcended all human barriers of class and race. These missionaries were witnesses—witnesses to Jesus through whom these infinite possibilities had been realized and apart from whom the Church itself would be inexplicable.

For the Christianity which eventually won the Roman empire was no logical evolution from the paganism of the Mediterranean world nor from the Judaism to which it owed so much; it was a fresh irruption, a new beginning which finds its centre and meaning in the person of Christ.

I

The Growth of the Church

IF, TO Christians, the growth of the Church is primarily
explicable in terms of supernatural power manifesting itself
in human life and in the realm of human history, this is not to
say that there were not factors in the contemporary situation
which favoured the spread of this new religion. They help in
part to explain its growth from a handful of men in a Jerusalem
street to a vast empire-embracing organization strong enough
to weather the onslaughts of the barbarians by which the
political might of Rome was ultimately brought down in
ruins. But even here the Christian will see the providential
arrangement of God in sending his Christ 'in the fulness of
the times', i.e. when the time was ripe.

What then were these factors?

First and most obvious was the existence of Rome itself.
Under a series of capable and energetic rulers the political
unity of the nations bordering on the Mediterranean had been
achieved. The effect of the consequent absence of strife and
the prevalence of the *pax Romana* on the spread of Christianity
has been conveniently summarized for us by the great Christian
scholar Origen. In his defence of Christianity against Celsus,
written in A.D. 246, he states:

There is abundance of peace which began at the birth of Christ,
God preparing the nations for his teaching, that they might be

under one prince, the king of the Romans, and that it might not be more difficult, owing to the lack of unity between the nations due to the existence of many kingdoms, for Jesus' apostles to accomplish the task laid upon them by their Master, when he said: 'Go and teach all nations.' Now the existence of many kingdoms would have been a hindrance to the preaching of the doctrine of Jesus throughout the entire world because of men everywhere engaging in war, and fighting for their native country, which was the case before Augustus, and in periods still more remote.

This unprecedented era of peace encouraged the growth of commerce and the development of communications. The Romans remain justly famous for their roads and when we note that in Britain alone over five thousand miles are known to have been laid during the occupation, we shall have some idea of the gigantic construction work undertaken and the immense facilitation of travel which ensued. It is not surprising therefore to learn, from the inscription on his tomb, that one Phrygian merchant journeyed to Rome no less than seventy-two times in the course of his life. The trade routes indeed provided highways for the advance of Christian teaching.

But the communication of this teaching would have been rendered exceedingly difficult had it not been for another important factor. The conquests of Alexander the Great had carried the Greek culture, and with it its language, far beyond the borders of his native land. Greek had indeed become the common tongue of the empire, so that wherever a Christian missionary went, to Spain, to North Africa or even to Rome itself, he could be sure that any audience he might collect would be able to understand what he had to say.

There were other factors too which ensured that he would have a not unsympathetic hearing. At the dawn of the Christian era, traditional religion had largely collapsed. The breakdown of the city states had led to a lack of local patriotism and a disregard for the local gods. The Olympian deities were no longer regarded with respect. Amusing and salacious though the stories about them may be, the love affairs of Zeus for example, his turning into a shower of gold to seduce Danae and into a bull to rape Europa, rendered him and his companions morally contemptible. It did not require the strictures of a Christian apologist to convince people of the impropriety of worshipping such beings and many would have agreed whole-heartedly with Athenagoras (A.D. 143) when he speaks of

how Kronos, for instance, castrated his father, and hurled him down from his chariot, and how he murdered his children, and swallowed the males of them; and how Zeus bound his father, and cast him down to Tartarus, as did Ouranus also to his sons, and fought with the Titans for the government; and how he persecuted his mother Rhea when she refused to wed him, and, she becoming a she-dragon, and he himself being changed into a dragon, bound her with what is called the Herculean knot, and accomplished his purpose, of which fact the rod of Hermes is a symbol; and again, how he violated his daughter Persephone, in this case also assuming the form of a dragon, and became the father of Dionysius. In face of narrations like these, I must say at least this much, what that is becoming or useful is there in such a history that we must believe them to be gods?

Into the religious void created by the rejection of, or at least the refusal to take seriously, these gods came the concept of Fate.

Throughout the whole world [declares Pliny, who was born in A.D. 23], at every place and hour, by every voice, Fortune alone is invoked and her name spoken: she is the one defendant, the one culprit, the one thought in men's minds, the one object of praise, the one cause. She is worshipped with insults, counted as fickle and often as blind, wandering, inconsistent, elusive, changeful, and friend of the unworthy. We are so much at the mercy of chance that Chance is our god.

The arbiters of this Fate, so it was believed, were the heavenly bodies, the planets and the stars, which controlled man's unalterable destiny. Astrology thus enjoyed great popularity and not a few emperors had in their permanent employ those who could cast their horoscopes. There was thus an acute sense of hopelessness and an ardent desire for release from one's seemingly inescapable plight. Accompanying this was widespread superstition. Men recounted tales of werewolves, of witches who beat folk to death, of hobgoblins who favoured some and hounded others. Man was at the mercy of evil spirits who could ruin his health and destroy his soul; countless secret foes were constantly attacking and possessing their defenceless victims.

In such a situation the message of a saviour was sure of a ready hearing and the mystery cults, such as those of Cybele, Serapis and Mithras, attracted many with the offer of salvation through a god who died and rose again. Typical of the attitude of their adherents is the prayer of Apuleius (early second century A.D.): 'Thine hand alone can disentangle the hopelessly knotted skeins of Fate, terminate every spell of bad weather, and restrain the stars from harmful conjunction.' Apuleius himself had been initiated according to the rites of Isis and Osiris; he had identified himself with the deity and undergone twelve emblematic transformations as he passed through the successive Houses of the Zodiac before undergoing his ritual death and rebirth. But these cults could not answer the widespread need, holding as they did that the favour of heaven was reserved for the wellborn and well educated. The majority of the population had neither the intelligence nor the discretion to qualify for initiation and only a limited number could afford to pay the high fees demanded. From some women were entirely excluded and all laid such stress on a dualism of body and soul, the former being the gloomy prison-house of the latter, that they made no appeal to the whole man.

Christianity gradually outstripped these rivals. With its powerful and coherent structure, its inclusiveness which disregarded barriers of race and class, its fixed principles and at the same time its readiness to adjust itself to current intellectual ideas and popular practices, it spread steadily and surely through the length and breadth of the empire. It supplied the religious hunger; it lifted men from the depths of the moral degradation into which contemporary pagan society had plunged them; it brought assurance of a personal Redeemer who would liberate them from evil and from death itself; through its exorcists it set people free from demon possession; through its rites of unction and the laying on of hands it cared for the sick; through its closely knit and genuine fellowship it provided a means of community life at a time when society was disintegrating. The religious vitality of its exponents, the nobleness of their lives, the mutual love of its adherents—all made an indelible impression upon those who came into contact with it. If the conversion of the emperor Constantine in the early fourth century served to give the Church a further impetus, it was but the hastening of a certain consummation.

Yet however much the factors which have been listed may help us to understand the growth and eventual triumph of the Church, they are insufficient apart from the key figure of Christ and the fulfilment of his promise that his Spirit would accompany and assist his followers to accomplish the task he had set them. If the supernatural did not come down to humble nature in the Bethlehem stable, if that which is beyond time did not enter time and abide with and in men in the upper room in Jerusalem, the Church remains an unsolved riddle.

·   ·   ·   ·   ·

From generalities let us turn to personalities. Who were the people who carried the message of salvation through the Graeco-Roman world and what were they like?

Tradition has it that after the Ascension of Christ, the twelve Apostles assembled at Jerusalem and 'distributed the regions of the world, that every one of them should go into the region that fell to him'. This, however, is no more than a pious fiction: there is no evidence of systematized planning and there is evidence that much of the early missionary work was both haphazard and fortuitous. The little group of Christians in Jerusalem soon found themselves at odds with the Jewish authorities, who had no more sympathy with them than they had had with their executed leader. Matters came to a head when Stephen, who asserted that they had been the betrayers and murderers of the Messiah, was stoned and a persecution broke out from which many of the faithful took refuge by flight, some going as far as Phoenicia and Cyprus. 'They therefore that were scattered abroad went about preaching the word.' These nameless missionaries are typical of the early history of the growth of Christianity; with but few exceptions it is some hundreds of years before the names of individual evangelists and the organization of their efforts are recorded. Outstanding among these exceptions was Paul of Tarsus.

According to the Acts of the Apostles, from which the detail concerning the outcome of Stephen's martyrdom has just been noted and which goes on to record the work of Philip in Samaria, we learn how this remarkable man was converted while on the way to Damascus to persecute the Christians there. After several years Paul himself set out to preach the faith he had once bitterly attacked; but before he did so he had to resolve two acute problems of missionary policy. To whom was the Gospel to be preached and on what terms were those who responded to it to be received into the Church?

The first Christians were Jews. Their acceptance of Jesus as Messiah did not immediately seem to them to involve any break with the nation or with their inherited beliefs. They continued to worship in the synagogue, to attend the Temple services and to observe the precepts of the Law. Their answers to the questions just formulated were quite direct: the Gospel is to be preached to the Jews first, then to the Gentiles who are to be received into the Church on condition that they become Jews and observe the Law. Paul was one of those—he was not the only one—who fought against this narrow exclusivism. He saw that Christianity was either a religion for all mankind or it was nothing. The Gospel was to be preached to everyone, and each and every one could accept it as the gracious gift of God. All that was required was faith, that is simple trust in God, self-committal to the One who had revealed his love in his Son. No other conditions, such as circumcision or the observance of the Sabbath or of food regulations, were necessary—indeed they were but a hindrance to the spread of the good news.

This was not a position which Paul found it easy to adopt. 'A Hebrew of Hebrews, as touching the Law, a Pharisee . . . as touching the righteousness which is in the law, found blameless,' he could only deny the necessity for converts observing the Law when he had himself evaluated it in a new light. Accordingly he taught that the Law was not an end in itself; it was an interim dispensation which was to reveal sin in its true colours and appraise men of their helplessness, thus serving as a preparatory discipline to make them ready for the coming of the Saviour. Its function was therefore to act as a 'tutor to bring us unto Christ'. Having served its purpose it was no longer authoritative and was to be regarded as having occupied only a temporary place in the religious history of mankind. Consequently, when he set out on his missionary journeys Paul was ready to deliver his message to anyone who would listen and he would lay no burden upon them save belief in the Lord Jesus and baptism in his name. The future lay with Paul, and the Jewish Christians who refused to break the bonds of their nationalism declined in numbers to the status of a sect, known as the Ebionites, and eventually disappeared from the pages of history.

It was probably in A.D. 46 that Paul and Barnabas were commissioned by the church at Antioch. Taking ship at nearby Seleucia, they sailed to Cyprus and then on to Perga; up the river valley to Antioch of Pisidia, and thence to Iconium, Lystra and Derbe in the central parts of Asia Minor. In each place the same procedure was followed. The campaign began with a visit to the local synagogue where an invitation was invariably issued to deliver an address, during the course of which Paul was able to declare that Jesus was the Messiah. Of his hearers, some welcomed the news, some asked for further information and discussion, some were immediately hostile. In face of the opposition of this third group, Paul then turned to the Gentiles only to be finally expelled through the influence of the leading Jews with the civic authorities. He and Barnabas then went on to the next place, leaving behind them a little nucleus of Christians to carry on the work of building up the Church.

The following year the two were back at their base in Syrian Antioch, and then in A.D. 50 Paul set off again, this time accompanied by Silas. Taking the overland route, he revisited those centres where he had already planted the seeds of the faith on his first journey and then pressed onwards directed, according to the record, by the Holy Spirit who on one occasion forbade him to proceed into the province of Asia and on another into that of Bithynia and so brought him eventually to the seaport of Troas on the Aegean coast. It was here that Paul had a vision summoning him to Macedonia; he embarked accordingly, landing at Neapolis and proceeding immediately to Philippi, and so down the coast to Athens and finally to Corinth. The round trip was completed by boat first to Ephesus, then to Caesarea and so back to Antioch.

The third missionary journey (A.D. 53–56) followed a similar route. Overland to encourage and help the growing churches; a prolonged stay at Ephesus; a visit to Corinth, a return through Macedonia and finally a sea voyage to Tyre and so up to Jerusalem, carrying the contributions from the Gentile believers towards the support of the Christian poor in the capital—a visible demonstration of the reality of the union of Jew and Gentile in the one Church.

There is no need to give fuller details of these journeys—they are graphically described in the Book of Acts, partly with the aid of the travel diary of one of Paul's companions, and they have been retold many times since. They were certainly not without incident—there is the local pagan priest taking Barnabas for Jupiter and Paul for Mercury on their first visit to Lystra; the imprisonment at Philippi or the near riot instigated by the silversmiths of Ephesus who saw in the success of Paul's preaching a threat to their trade of making shrines for the goddess Diana. Of the cost to Paul and his helpers in effort and in suffering we may gain some understanding from the apostle's own words:

I have five times received the regulation thirty-nine stripes beating from the Jews. I was flogged three times. I have spent a night and day in the open sea. I have often been in considerable danger from rivers, robbers, among my own countrymen, and the

Gentiles. I have faced danger in the city, in the desert, on the sea, and among false Christians. I have known exhaustion, sleepless watchings, hunger and thirst, often without a meal, sometimes cold and without clothing. And in addition to all this, there is the constant daily care for all the churches.

And this was written before the final visit to Jerusalem, where, about to be lynched by the crowd, as Stephen had been before him, he was arrested on the false charge of profaning the Temple, was held in custody for two years at Caesarea, and was taken under armed escort to Rome, being shipwrecked once more before being brought to the imperial city.

But Paul allowed nothing to deflect him from the vocation which he believed had been laid upon him. 'Woe is unto me, if I preach not the Gospel.' To this end he made use of every opportunity that presented itself. He did not confine himself to a single method of approach and if he usually began in the synagogue, he was ready at Athens to speak in the market place like any wandering philosopher and at Ephesus to hire a lecture-room and give daily instruction. On the steps of the Antonia Tower, immediately after his arrest, in the midst of the supreme legislative assembly of the Jews, the Sanhedrin, before the proconsuls Felix and Festus and before Herod Agrippa and his queen Berenice at Caesarea, at the height of a storm in the Mediterranean, on the island of Malta after swimming through the breakers from the foundering ship— no matter where he was, Paul preached the Gospel. There is every reason to suppose that if his appeal was heard by the emperor in person, there too the apostle gave his witness, paying finally with his life for his steadfast adherence to the Lord whom he was sure he had met on the Damascus road.

With the death of Paul the curtain falls on the detailed scene of Christian missionary endeavour. We know that Barnabas and John Mark went to Cyprus, that Peter visited

Antioch, Corinth and Rome, but no account remains of the countless Christian men and women who carried on with the work of evangelization. The chief agents in the expansion of the Church were not those who made it their sole profession, but those who worked at a trade and spoke to their fellow workers and neighbours. If Justin Martyr († 163–7) gave public lectures in Rome, most made use of private contacts and even trade contacts. Just as Paul converted Aquila and Prisca, tent-makers like himself with whom he worked to gain a livelihood while still carrying on his preaching, so some hundred and twenty years later Celsus could complain of workers in wool and leather and fullers who laid hold of women and children to instruct them in the rudiments of the Christian faith. But Christians evangelized not only by word of mouth but also by their manner of life and so Justin speaks of the many pagans who 'have changed their violent and tyrannical disposition, being overcome either by the constancy which they have witnessed in the lives of their Christian neighbours, or by the extraordinary forbearance they have observed in their Christian fellow travellers when defrauded, and by the honesty of those believers with whom they have transacted business'.

The dearth of evidence is tantalizing to the extreme. The early history of the Church in any one area is not only fragmentary but frequently non-existent. Thus the first information we have of Christianity in Gaul is contained in a letter, written in A.D. 177, by the Christians of Lyons and Vienne to their fellow believers in Asia and Phrygia. This records the bloody persecution of the local church when many, from Blandina the slave-girl to Pothinus the bishop, were martyred. We may speculate on the origins of this thriving little community to the effect that as Gaul had close commercial relations with the eastern Mediterranean the faith had been most probably brought by traders from Asia Minor who had penetrated, past Marseilles, up the river Rhône—but when this took place and what persons were involved is not and probably will never be known. Again in North Africa which was to have such a virile Christianity and to boast such names as Tertullian, Cyprian and Augustine, it is not until A.D. 180 that evidence is forthcoming as to the existence of the Church in the form of the minutes of the court which on July 17th condemned twelve men and women of Scili in Numidia as Christians and ordered them to be beheaded. Intimate commercial connexions with Rome might suggest that the springboard of African evangelization was the imperial city, but by whom and when we have no means of telling. Even the origins of the Church in Rome itself are entirely obscure. When Paul wrote his letter to the Romans (about A.D. 56), it was already a powerful and respected community, but of its previous history there is no trace.

Nevertheless, if details are lacking it is possible to sketch in the broad outlines of the development. In the place of its origin, Palestine, the Church made little initial headway. As late as the fourth century the local community in Jerusalem was numerically so weak that it could not obtain possession of the site of the holy sepulchre, and even by A.D. 400 many places were still essentially pagan. But to the north in Syria the faith early gained a secure foothold. Antioch, the third city of the empire, where the followers of Christ first received the name of Christian, had many believers amongst its population, and indeed by the second half of the third century they were sufficiently influential for their bishop to be appointed as a high state official, and by the end of the fourth century there were several churches in the city, the total of those members attending the principal one being recorded as 100,000. But the Christian country *par excellence* in the pre-Constantinian era was Asia Minor, where Paul had done much of the spadework. Others followed in his footsteps in the Greek cities along the coast and up the valleys and within fifty years of his death the Church was to be found in almost every province. The advance continued steadily, so for example in the report of Pliny, governor of Bithynia, to his imperial master Trajan, c. 112, we read: 'the contagion of this superstition has spread not only through the free cities, but to the villages and rural districts', while of Pontus we are informed that when Gregory Thaumaturgus was made bishop, c. A.D. 240, there were only seventeen Christians in his diocese, but at his death, some twenty-five years later, only that number of pagans remained.

Across the Aegean, in what is now the modern Bulgaria, there were many churches before the fourth century, but in the south, apart from such centres as Thessalonica and Corinth, Christianity did not at first become acclimatized, although it had achieved a firm footing by the fifth century, especially in Dalmatia, where a wealth of inscriptions reveals a prospering community, and at Salona, where there is a Christian cemetery dating from the very beginning of the second century.

In Italy Rome overshadowed all other centres. By A.D. 257 the number of Christians was in the region of 30,000, and the emperor Decius (249–51) declared that he would rather have a rival emperor in Rome than a Christian bishop. In southern Italy the catacombs at Naples witness to an important community as early as the second century, while in the north the ports of Classis and Aquileia allowed ready access of Christian ideas from the East.

In Gaul, to which reference has already been made, the western districts were little touched by Christianity before the fourth century, but by the council of Arles in 314 bishoprics had been created in all parts. It was not however until after A.D. 450 that Gaul, i.e. its Roman population, became substantially Christian.

There were also present at Arles, besides the native clergy, three bishops from Britain, but little is known of the previous history of the Church there when it was no more than a military province with a veneer of Roman culture. It was only in the fourth century that Britain became christianized to any large extent, and then consequent upon the barbarian invasions it was cut off from the rest of Christendom in the middle of the next century, the last recorded British visit to Rome being made by Patrick about 441 to obtain Leo's support for his mission to Ireland. In the interval that elapsed before the arrival of Augustine in 597 the Celtic Church, stimulated by Druidic competition, became first in Wales and then in Ireland a centre of sturdy intellectual life, producing many missionaries to bring Britain back to the faith. Such men as Ninian in Galloway or Columba in Yorkshire and Durham have had their equals but not their superiors as preachers of the Gospel by word and example.

The history of the Spanish Church begins with the third century when a letter from Cyprian reveals that there were Christians at Leon, Astorga, Merida and Saragossa. The only other source of information is the canons of the Council of Elvira (c. A.D. 303) which indicate that Christianity was widely diffused.

North-west Africa, the fertile strip of land between the sea and the range of mountains, was a second Italy and the granary of Rome. Evidence for the existence of the Church there is forthcoming from the end of the second century, but it was in the following century that the most spectacular advance took place and something like a mass movement into the Church occurred. Unfortunately it was mainly the settlers of Italian origin that were affected; the Punic element in the Church only became strong in the fourth century, while the indigenous Berber population was hardly touched and this in part explains the almost total disappearance of Christianity after the later Mohammedan invasions. Before these onslaughts the province had already been overrun by the Arian

Vandals, 429–39, but was regained for Justinian by the romantic figure Belisarius in 535 and remained a Byzantine province until the end of the seventh century.

That the Church survived the invasions in Egypt is probably due to the fact that the native population was largely converted. The Coptic or peasant stock embraced the faith in large numbers and the presence of Christians even in the remote villages of the interior is shown by the *libelli* or certificates of having sacrificed during the Decian persecution which have been found among Egyptian papyri. But fifty years before this Alexandria itself had become a great centre of Christian scholarship, with a flourishing school under the successive headships of Pantaenus, Clement and Origen.

We have now completed a round tour of the Mediterranean basin and seen the Church advancing in all areas. Exact statistics are impossible where the evidence is so fragmentary but most estimates give the proportion of Christians as ranging from one-twentieth to one-eighth of the population of the Roman empire. The Church, however, even in this pre-Constantinian period, was not so geographically confined. In the third century the kingdom of Armenia was penetrated and Tiridates III was converted *c.* A.D. 280 through the efforts of Gregory the Illuminator. By 316, the year of the king's death, Armenia was mainly a Christian country. Mesopotamia too heard of the faith before the mid-second century from Addai, a Palestinian Jew, who was subsequently confused with the apostle Thaddeus. At the turn of the century the royal house, in the person of Abgar IX, joined the Church, and Edessa became the headquarters of a missionary movement designed to convert the rural districts of Syria. It was also from Edessa that the Gospel was carried further east to Nisibis and so on to Persia, where the extensive persecutions of the fourth century indicate the continued growth of Christianity. Hence Constantine's letter to King Sapur: 'I am delighted to hear that the finest districts of Persia also are adorned with the presence of Christians.' It is even possible that before the end of the third century Christianity had arrived in India, for there were connexions between that country and Rome largely through Alexandria.

The growth of the Church, which even the protracted persecutions could not halt, was greatly accelerated through the conversion of Constantine. Christianity now received the support of the government, becoming eventually the official State religion. Before long the emperors themselves were leading the attack upon the pagan cults, first withdrawing the privileges they enjoyed and then actively seeking to stamp them out. Something of the delight this must have afforded the faithful is revealed by a sketch on the wall of a subterranean chamber in the cemetery of Hermes on the *Via Salaria vetus* at Rome. The unknown doodler—he was certainly no artist—has drawn in charcoal a figure on a pedestal with a sceptre in one hand; to its right there is a person throwing stones and to its left a man pulling a rope which is fastened around the statue's neck. But the many whom this freedom from repression brought into the Church were not all of the quality of previous converts. Some were baptized as a matter of policy; some under official pressure; others because their friends and neighbours were so doing. The effect of this upon the inner life of the Church was by no means negligible and we shall see in a later chapter what steps were taken to raise its spiritual temper.

But despite the more congenial circumstances in which the Church was now labouring, it was not content merely to bask in the imperial favour nor to live upon its spiritual capital inherited from former generations. A not insignificant number of outstanding men entered the ministry and, amongst other tasks, conceived it their duty to seek to bring all in the areas under their care to Christ. So in Gaul, Martin, a one-time soldier, who became bishop of Tours in 372, set out to convert systematically the whole of the surrounding pagan countryside, preaching, destroying temples and baptizing. In northern Italy Ambrose, who from the lofty office of provincial governor had become bishop of Milan in 373, encouraged by letter missions in the Tyrol which were under the direct supervision of Vigilius, later second bishop of Brescia. In North Africa, Augustine, bishop of Hippo from *c.* 395, wrote innumerable letters expounding the faith to pagans; he worked out a carefully graded system of instructions for converts and encouraged his clergy to make as many contacts with non-Christians as possible. From Constantinople John Chrysostom (consecrated in 398) sent parties of monks to destroy pagan temples; he commissioned a bishop for the Goths, and when, through the disfavour of the emperor, he was exiled to the Caucasus he continued to encourage missions in Cilicia and Phoenicia. Itinerant missionaries were not unknown and a certain Philaster travelled the length and breadth of the empire, winning many by private and public disputations, before becoming bishop of Brescia.

The motives which brought folk into the Church were not always of the highest. So in the early fifth century there is a report of pagans converted in Gaul because a cattle plague spared the animals owned by Christians. From the Church historian Sozomen we learn that his grandfather and all his family embraced the faith because of hearing of the cure of a demon-possessed man through calling on the name of Christ. But Chrysostom was of the opinion, and many would have agreed with him, that the most effective means was the example of Christian living. 'There would be no more heathens,' he said, 'if we would be true Christians.' However varied and complex the motives, suffice it to say now that by the year 500, after a bitter struggle with the old cults and against some of the new ones such as Manichaeism, the great majority of the population of the empire called themselves Christians. This however is not the complete picture, for not only did the Church continue to push forward outside the boundaries of the empire, but the empire itself, due to the invasions of the Germanic tribes, underwent a considerable transformation.

Outside the boundaries, Christianity advanced in the north into Georgia, in the south-east into Arabia and in the south as far as Abyssinia. Of this last advance Socrates has preserved the story which may well contain trustworthy details. A certain Tyrian philosopher named Meropius set off on a voyage down the Red Sea, accompanied by two young men who were his relations. Touching at a port on the African coast to obtain supplies, the whole ship's company was massacred by the local inhabitants except for the two youths. One of them, Aedisius, was made the king's cup-bearer and the other, Frumentius, was entrusted with the care of the royal records. The latter, having acquired a position of some importance, undertook the spiritual care of Christian merchants visiting the city and built a church for them. Eventually he was allowed to go to Alexandria (c. 355), where Athanasius consecrated him bishop, and he returned to the country of his adoption to continue his missionary work. Yet it was not these small advances that were to prove of most significance for the Church during the next thousand years—the all-important factor was the wave after wave of northern tribes which swept over the Roman empire.

In the year 410 the Visigoths, who had moved from the north of the Danube, invaded Italy under Alaric and captured Rome. 'The whole world has perished in one city,' declared Jerome when the news reached him in Bethlehem. But this was only the beginning. From Germany the Vandals were pressing down into Gaul and in 409 crossed the Pyrenees. Hard on their heels came the Visigoths, who had withdrawn from Italy, and driving the Vandals before them across the Mediterranean into North Africa, they set up a kingdom in Spain. Fast behind them came the Franks from Belgium, bringing all Gaul under their sway. Into Italy again, in the last decade of the fifth century, came the Ostrogoths from south of the Danube, only to give way in the next century to the Lombards. In the seventh century the Slavs, who had established themselves in central Europe, poured over the Balkans. The whole pattern of political order was continuously in a ferment, and it would not have been surprising had the Church, so closely identified by now with the Roman state, to such an extent that the Persians attacked Christians because theirs was the religion of the empire, gone down in the general ruin. That it did not do so was in part due to the vitality of the Christian religion and in part to the fact that many of the invading tribes did not so much wish to destroy Rome as to succeed to its splendour. So according to Ataulf, who led the Visigoths from Italy into Gaul:

At first I longed to destroy and beat down the Roman empire, but after I had learnt from experience that the Goths, because of their unbridled savagery, could not obey laws, I chose instead to seek the glory of restoring completely the Roman name and of buttressing it by using the strength of the Goths in the hope that later ages might know of me as the restorer of Rome.

In this restoration the Church was regarded as having a necessary place, all the more so as many of the tribes had already heard something of the Gospel.

It seems likely that Christianity was first brought to the Goths by slaves captured during their periodic raids across the Roman frontier. But the chief architect of the Gothic Church was a man, probably of the same race, named Ulfilas, who in 341, at the age of thirty, was consecrated bishop 'of the

Christians in Gothia', and worked among the people north of the Danube. To him belongs the distinction of having devised an alphabet and of translating a large part of the Bible into Gothic—being thus the precursor of many other missionaries who have since accomplished the same tasks in other parts of the world. His Christianity however was of the heretical brand known as Arianism and part of the history of the next centuries is the story of how, settled in southern Gaul and Spain, the spiritual descendants of Ulfilas were brought over to orthodoxy. It is from these Visigoths that the Ostrogoths and Vandals would appear to have received their faith. The Franks on the other hand were predominantly pagan and it was not until after they had established themselves in Gaul that, under Clovis, they were brought into the Church following the king's baptism on December 25th, 496. As the founder of what was to become the most important of the kingdoms which in the West succeeded the Roman empire, numbering among his descendants Charles the Great ruling over the Carolingian empire, Clovis was an essential link in preserving a large area of the old empire for the Christian faith.

So the scene is set for the next advance of the Church, which was to be not so much an extensive movement as an intensive one concerned to bring these tribes, now nominally Christian, under the civilizing and humanizing yoke of the Gospel. In the future still lay the capturing of northern Europe for Christ and the labours of Boniface among the tribes east of the Rhine, but the movement was well under way. The storm of political upheaval had been weathered, and the Church was firmly set on its course with only the weakness of its human components to delay its success.

2

The Structure of the Church

ON NOVEMBER 3RD, 361, a mystical phil-Hellene named Julian ascended the imperial throne. Disposed to be anti-Christian by the circumstances of his youth and upbringing, he set himself to re-establish the worship of the ancient gods. His methods, however, were not those of the persecuting emperors of the third century. 'He employed a gentle violence,' comments Jerome, 'which strove to win and not to drive.' Foremost amongst his projects was the creation of a Holy Catholic Church of Hellenism and to this end he took the office of Pontifex Maximus and organized an elaborate hierarchy beneath him. Each province had its high priest with jurisdiction over all the priests in his area. These offices were to be held for life, and so the old system whereby leading laymen undertook priestly duties for a year and then retired was superseded. Julian was also concerned to infuse into this ministry a high moral tone. Accordingly he gave directions that they were to be charitable, grave and chaste; that they were not to frequent theatres or taverns or associate with jockeys and dancers; that they were to engage in regular fasting; that they were to recite prayers three times a day at fixed hours, making use of a psalter of pagan hymns, and that a sermon was to be included in all acts of worship. There is no need to continue this list of regulations, for sufficient items have been given to indicate that Julian was modelling his reformed paganism on the Christian Church, which it was to supersede, and thereby he testified to its effective and compelling power and to the high moral level of its average officers.

Yet Julian was not the first to recognize in the structure of the Church one of the reasons for its success. In the last quarter of the second century, a group of enthusiasts in Phrygia, known as the Montanists, broke away from the main body of the faithful, making exaggerated claims as to their direct inspiration by the Holy Spirit. They formed themselves into an organized group, with bishops, priests and deacons, on the model of the Church, to which were added patriarchs and certain ministers whose function is not described called the *koinonoi*. In the same period an heretical movement known as Marcionitism had its origin; this spread with great rapidity and one of the reasons for this was its careful organization, so that Tertullian (*fl. c.* 200) could compare its adherents to wasps busy making combs like bees but failing, unlike the genuine article, to produce true honey.

Here then are three unbiased testimonies, from Julian, the Montanists and the Marcionites, as to the importance of structure for the furtherance of the Gospel. It is now time to examine this structure more closely to illuminate the making of the Church.

At the outset emphasis must be laid upon the word 'structure' which is employed deliberately instead of 'organization'. The first Christians did not think of the Church primarily as an organized society; to them the Church meant the faithful Remnant who were heirs of the divine promises; it was the New Israel comprising God's elect; it was a Temple, built of living stones, in which the Holy Spirit was present; it was the Body of Christ, composed of innumerable cells, whose corporate task it was to grow in Christlikeness and to bring all mankind into unity with its Lord; it was the sphere of the new creation in which the barriers of sex, class, race and of sin were transcended. Above all, the Church was a divinely founded fellowship of those who had been 'enlightened and tasted of the heavenly gift, and were made partakers of the Holy Ghost, and tasted the good word of God, and the powers of the age to come'. It was not, therefore, a group of like-minded people concerned with God who had come together to form a society for the furtherance of their common religious interests, much as, for example, a number of those keen on dinghies might organize themselves into a sailing club. It was a divine-human organism established by the initiative and direct action of God in history, and its first members were unlikely to have been concerned with questions of constitutional order. Nevertheless the evidence is indisputable that from the second century the Church possessed an ordained ministry, consisting, at the top, of bishops, presbyters or priests and deacons. From whence was this element in its structure derived?

Two main theories have been propounded to answer this question—there are others but they are largely variations of these two. On the one hand there is the authoritarian theory—sometimes described as 'from above'—to the effect that Christ commissioned the twelve apostles to be his personal representatives; they in turn commissioned others—the bishops—to succeed them; each bishop is therefore a successor of the apostles or even an addition to the apostolic college, and stands in an unbroken line of succession reaching back to the Apostolic Age. On the other hand there is the democratic theory—sometimes described as 'from below'—to the effect that the Church is free to arrange its ministry to suit the circumstances of any age or clime and that no particular form of ministry, whether episcopal or presbyterian, is therefore essential.

The evidence at our disposal from the first generations of

the Church's history is fragmentary and ambiguous, and upholders of each theory have been able to interpret it, to their own satisfaction, as providing support for their position. To the present writer it seems well-nigh impossible to arrive at any certainty on historical grounds alone, and he is bound to affirm that he finds the antithesis, from above or below, unacceptable, since it passes over completely the all-important fact of the Spirit's presence in the Church. He sees the Apostolic Age as the embryonic period of the Church's existence when, under the moulding hand of the Spirit and not uninfluenced by such systems as the synagogue-ruler and his fellow elders or the situation at Jerusalem where James, the brother of Christ, seems to have taken the lead, the threefold ministry gradually emerged and assumed the character which it has preserved in many parts of Christendom ever since. These ministries are indeed functions, necessary to the life of the Church, which are performed by those who have received authority so to do, and this authority is that of the whole Church, and therefore of Christ through his Spirit in the Church, exercised through specific organs. With these considerations in mind, it is now possible to describe these ministries as they appear in the clear light of day from the beginning of the second century onwards.

The corner-stone of the structure was the bishop. He entered upon his function, after election by the people—acclamation and not show of hands or voting papers being the method used—and after consecration by the laying on of hands of his fellow bishops, of whom the number had to be, according to the Council of Nicaea (325), not less than three. His principal duties are conveniently summarized in the prayer preserved in the *Apostolic Tradition* (c. 217):

Grant unto this thy servant whom thou hast chosen for the episcopate to feed thy holy flock, and to exercise the High-priesthood before thee, without blame to serve thee day and night, unceasingly to propitiate thy countenance and to offer the gifts of thy holy Church; endued with the high priestly spirit to have power to forgive sins according to thy command, confer orders according to thy precept, and to loose every bond according to the authority thou didst give unto the Apostles, and to be well-pleasing unto thee in meekness and cleanness of heart.

The bishop had therefore, first, 'to feed thy holy flock'. This involved the constant surveillance of the spiritual welfare of the people to whom he was to act as a true shepherd and a father in God. He had to visit the sick; he had to look after the poor, paying particular attention to the unprotected widows and orphans. He had therefore to administer the finances of the church over which he had been placed. In the earliest days the main source of this money was the freewill offerings of the faithful, and so Justin informs us: 'what is collected is deposited with the president, who succours the orphans and widows, and those who, through sickness or any other cause, are in want, and those who are in bonds, and the strangers staying among us, and in a word takes care of all that are in need'. In course of time with the growth of the Church and with the imperial favour which began in the fourth century, the revenues increased considerably, so that in addition to the regular offerings there were various properties which, under a law of Constantine, it became possible to bequeath to the Church; further there were the estates of martyrs and of clergy dying intestate, a regular allowance from the imperial exchequer, as well as tithes and first fruits. Consequently it became customary for a bishop, in later times, to be assisted by a steward. That this was no small task may be seen from the fact that by A.D. 400 the Christian Church in Constantinople numbered some 100,000 and they made themselves responsible for the maintenance of 50,000 poor folk.

The second function of the bishop specified in the prayer quoted above was 'to offer the gifts of thy holy Church'. This refers to the celebration of the sacraments and of the Eucharist in particular, and, closely connected with this, the preaching of the sermon. The bishop was in fact the primary liturgical minister and others only undertook this duty as his delegates.

Thirdly, the bishop was 'to forgive sins'—a reference to the granting of absolution with which is to be closely associated the system of discipline that gradually evolved. It lay within his power to impose penance and to excommunicate, and to confer with his fellow bishops on regulations for the well-being of the Church at large. He was also expected, from the earliest days, to hear and settle secular and civil cases in accordance with Paul's injunction that the faithful were not to go to law before unbelievers. This episcopal jurisdiction was given state recognition in the fourth century, and not a little of the bishop's time was taken up with it. According to the *Apostolic Constitutions* (c. 400) the cases were to be tried usually on a Monday morning in order that, should any controversy arise about the decision, it might be dealt with before the following Sunday and the parties be set at peace with one another.

As an illustration of the kind of problem with which the bishop had to cope we may take a case which was heard before Ambrose of Milan in 378. The brother of a certain bishop applied for the annulment of an agreement whereby the bishop had granted one of his family estates to their widowed sister on condition that it should pass on her death to the Church. The bishop however was a decurion and it was forbidden by law for one in such a position to sell or alienate his goods and property without the authorization of the prefect, since his hereditary membership of the curia involved heavy expenses which had to be met. The bishop's legal heir was his own brother who would succeed him as a decurion and would have to bear the heavy expenses. The accused argued that by a law of 361 it was enacted that all clergy who were decurions, with the exception of those consecrated to the episcopacy, should forfeit their possessions upon ordination, so that as bishop he retained full rights over his patrimony. The plaintiff replied that the law did not state that a bishop had the right to dispose of his property in such a way that it ceased to be available for the charges of the curia. Ambrose's decision was that the land in question was to be given to the brother who was to make an annual payment to the sister; after her decease, he could continue possession of the estate without obligation to further payment to the Church. The plaintiff thus received the land; the sister was assured of a fixed income for life, and the defendant was relieved of an unfortunate dissension in his family. The only loser was the Church who, according to Ambrose, could afford to dispense with temporal gains.

Finally the bishop was to 'confer orders', i.e. he was the primary minister of ordination, although in the ordination of presbyters other presbyters were associated with him. It is also to be noted that the bishop was the minister of confirmation, but in the East this was eventually delegated to the presbyters who made use of oil episcopally blessed.

Although the presbyterate was eventually to form the backbone of the Church, insofar as its members became the parish priests of the mediaeval and modern periods, in the first centuries its role was somewhat passive and indeed it is not easy to differentiate it from the episcopate. This arises from the fact that, with the sole exception of ordination, a presbyter could perform all the functions of a bishop. Nevertheless he did so only as the bishop's deputy. 'Let that Eucharist be considered valid,' states Ignatius († c. 114), 'which is under the bishop or him to whom he commits it'. The presbyter did not therefore teach, baptize or celebrate except insofar as he had the bishop's express permission to do so.

This liturgical dependence of the one upon the other may be illustrated from an interesting custom which survived in the West until the eighth and ninth centuries, although in the East it dropped out of use by the fourth. This was the practice of conveying a portion of the bread consecrated by the bishop at the Eucharist over which he was presiding to be placed in the chalice at each of the lesser Eucharists celebrated by the presbyters elsewhere in the same city. This *fermentum*, as it was termed, was a token that the bishop was the high priest and liturgical minister of his whole church and that each presbyter was at the same time in union with him and subordinate to him.

The presbyter was then subject to the bishop who could call him to account, whereas he and his fellow presbyters could not censure their superior. At the same time the presbyters did assist in the government of the Church, forming a kind of senate or council under episcopal presidency. It was indeed seldom that a bishop acted without seeking their advice and so in the ordination prayer of the *Apostolic Tradition* the petition is made that the presbyter might be filled 'with the spirit of grace and counsel . . . and govern thy people with a pure heart'.

If the functions of the presbyter are not very clearly defined, because he was largely a shadow of the bishop, those of the deacon were much more precise. He was the bishop's right-hand man, so much so that in one document he is referred to as the ears, eyes, heart and mouth of the bishop and even as his soul and perception. It was the deacon who was the main channel of communication between the bishop and the laity. All offerings were made through his hands and he acted, under the bishop, as the steward of church property and almoner of charitable undertakings. It was his task to seek out those that were sick and give a list of their names to his superior. He it was who examined the letters commendatory carried by visiting Christians and he was frequently entrusted with embassies to foreign parts. The deacon too acted as a disciplinary officer under episcopal direction: he had to discover and reprimand offenders, to strengthen the faint-hearted and encourage the waverers, and to deal with the less complex cases which came up for adjudication. His disciplinary duties overlapped with his liturgical, for at the Eucharist he was responsible for the maintenance of order, by circulating among the congregation to stop the whisperers and awake the sleepers. He had to stand by the door to prevent the entrance of unbelievers once the service proper had begun. At the actual celebration the deacon read the Gospel, summoned to prayer, dismissed the catechumens and penitents, presented the offerings of the people, gave the signal for the kiss of peace, administered the chalice, and, at the conclusion of the service, carried the reserved sacrament to those who had been unavoidably absent through sickness or other legitimate cause.

So manifold were the deacons' duties that the limitation of their number to seven in any one city, which was a general though by no means universal rule based upon the account in Acts 6 of the appointment of the Seven who were believed, on uncertain grounds, to have been the first deacons, meant that as congregations increased it became more and more impossible to do all that was required of them. To meet this situation further orders, which came to be known as the minor orders, were created, but before this took place on any large scale there was already in existence a group of lectors or readers.

At first the Church seems to have followed the practice of the Jewish synagogue according to which those in charge of the service could invite whomsoever they wished to read the lessons; but their choice must have been severely limited by the minority of those present who would be literate. Although there are references to the one that reads in the opening verses of the book of Revelation and in the account of Sunday worship given by Justin Martyr, it is not until Hippolytus († c. 236) that we have any indication of a definite order in his statement: 'the reader is appointed by the bishop giving him the book, for he is not ordained'. By the middle of the third century in Carthage the readers were numbered among the clergy, and Cyprian († 258) expressed the hope that a certain Aurelius, a confessor made reader, might merit 'higher degrees of clerical ordination', but, he adds, 'in the meantime I judged it well that he should begin with the office of reading'. A great number of ecclesiastics later began their careers in this way by serving a probationary period in the lectorate, e.g. Felix of Nola, Eusebius of Vercelli, popes Liberius and Siricius and many others.

The lector was initially responsible for reading all the lessons that formed part of the liturgy. At the time of Justin these included not only 'the memoirs of the Apostles' but also 'the writings of the prophets'. In the third century the lector read the Gospel but by the fourth he had lost this privilege to the deacon, and when in the sixth century the number of lessons was reduced to two, the lectorate became largely redundant. In this brief history of the readership we see the reverse of the process we are about to consider: in this case the order of readers did not derive from the diaconate and in course of time its function was absorbed by it. The other minor orders however did so originate as the name of the first—the subdiaconate—reveals.

The subdeacon is first mentioned in the *Apostolic Tradition*, and since its author, Hippolytus, was concerned not to innovate but to record the normal practices at Rome which he believed to be of apostolic origin, we have evidence for the practice of thirty or even fifty years earlier. The subdeacon must therefore have been in existence at Rome by A.D. 170–180. The same document provides us with an indication not only of date but also of the nature of the office, since it states:

'Hands shall not be laid upon a subdeacon, but his name shall be mentioned that he may serve the deacon.' The subdeacon therefore was an assistant to the deacon and exercised several of his functions. Thus, like the deacon, he had to 'be alert on the bishop's behalf' to inform him of any that were sick; he was employed in the carrying of letters, and while the deacon guarded the men's entrance to the church during the Eucharist he was on duty by the women's door. By the end of the fourth century the subdeacon was the overseer and keeper of God's holy vessels, and the bringer of water for the lavabo and ablutions. By the fifth century his ordination comprised the reception from the bishop of a ewer and a towel.

But even the help of the subdeacon was insufficient to relieve the pressure upon the deacon and so under bishop Fabian of Rome (236–50) three more orders were instituted, viz. acolytes, doorkeepers and exorcists.

The acolytes were employed to deliver letters and to distribute alms to the poor. They were not at first to be found in all churches in the West, the smaller ones having no need of them; so, e.g., at Rheims in the fifth century there were still no acolytes. Their importance eventually increased when they acquired certain liturgical functions, and we see the beginning of this in the fifth century when a canon affirms that at his ordination an acolyte is to receive a candlestick and a taper together with an empty cruet for the communion wine.

The doorkeeper took over the deacon's task of guarding the entrances during the Eucharist and by the fifth century his ordination consisted in the reception of a key. But the opening of the Church services to all who wished to attend made this duty redundant, and so in the sixth century the office became equivalent to that of a verger and the Council of Toledo in 597 declared that the doorkeeper had to provide for the cleaning and lighting of the church and sanctuary.

The exorcists were those whose task it was to care for the

energumens or demoniacs. The pitiful condition of these unfortunate people, whom in more modern though not necessarily more accurate parlance we should call the mentally deranged, has been vividly described by Cyprian: the evil spirits 'disturb their life; they disquiet their slumbers; creeping also into their bodies, they secretly terrify their minds, distort their limbs, break their health and feign diseases'. It was the task of the exorcist to visit them daily, to provide them with food and to lay his hands upon them. His primary function was therefore a pastoral one, derived in part from the diaconate whose normal responsibility it was to visit the sick.

In a letter of the year A.D. 251, which Cornelius of Rome sent to Fabius, bishop of Antioch, the writer had occasion to enumerate the clergy which were at that time officiating in the imperial capital. 'There are,' he states, 'one bishop, forty-six presbyters, seven deacons, seven subdeacons, forty-two acolytes, fifty-two exorcists, readers and doorkeepers.' As Rome had been recently divided into seven ecclesiastical regions, this meant that there was one deacon to each region, assisted by one subdeacon and six acolytes. Noticeably absent from this list is any mention of an order of women, although the Church did eventually have two such orders, one of widows and one of deaconesses.

There is no single period in the history of the early Church for which evidence of the existence of an order of widows is lacking. Even in the small community at Joppa widows formed a recognized body, as we learn from the account of Peter's visit there, while at Jerusalem they were so important that the dissatisfaction of a section of them could occupy the attention of the apostles themselves and led to the appointment of the Seven. So prominent a feature of Church life were they that even the outsider was aware of them, and Lucian in his satire of the faith could represent them as thronging the gate of the prison where the bogus Christian Peregrinus had been shut up. They were however in no sense an active order; rather they were an organized group of Church pensioners, and to be on the 'roll' was to be the recipient of charity. Throughout the second century this was their invariable characteristic, and so they were the special concern of the bishop and part of the offerings at the Eucharist were set aside for them. Their only function was that of intercession, and Hippolytus affirms that they are not ordained but are 'appointed for prayer, and prayer is the duty of all'.

In the third century a change took place and the *Didascalia* (*c.* 250), while mentioning them as the recipients of charity and the practitioners of intercession, declares that they should work at wool to give to those in distress and should visit the sick, laying their hands upon them and praying with them. According to the *Apostolic Church Ordinances* there are to be three widows in each congregation:

two to persevere in prayer for all those who are in temptation, and for the reception of revelations where such are necessary, but one to assist the women visited with sickness; she must be ready for service, discreet, communicating what is necessary to the presbyters, not avaricious, not given to much love of wine, so that she may be sober and capable of performing the night services, and other loving service if she will.

The third of this trio is almost indistinguishable, save in name, from a deaconess, and there is evidence that the order of deaconesses was recruited from groups of active widows. The primitive order of widows, as a body of Church pensioners, continued, but many now sought to serve the Church in a regularized form of ministry, which would appear to have come into existence in the first half of the third century, devolving from and therefore sharing certain restricted functions of the male diaconate. Here again, as was the case with the five minor orders, the principal cause of this development lay in the increased number of the faithful coupled with the strict seclusion of the female sex in Greece and in some oriental countries, thus necessitating a special ministry of women to them. The order of deaconesses was indeed an Eastern creation, being unknown in the West before the fifth century and only being accepted at Rome in the eighth.

The deaconess had certain precisely defined duties. According to the *Didascalia* she had to visit the sick women in those heathen households where a deacon might not fittingly enter. She had to administer the unction to women prior to their descent into the font. She received the female candidates after initiation and had to 'instruct them how the seal of baptism may be unbroken in chastity and holiness'. From later documents we learn that the deaconess took over the surveillance of the women's door and arranged their places in church, acted as the means of communication between all female members of the congregation and the bishop, and conveyed to sick women the reserved sacrament. She was in fact concerned exclusively with the women, so the *Didascalia* states that in the choice of deacons it is necessary to appoint 'a man for the performance of the most things that are required, but a woman for the ministry of women'. Similarly, according to Epiphanius:

though there is an order of deaconesses in the Church, yet it is not for priestly service, nor to undertake anything of the sort, but on account of the modesty of the female sex with a view to either the occasion of baptism, or of the inspection of illness, or of suffering, and when the woman's body is bared, so that it might not be seen by the men officiating, but by the deaconess, who is directed by the priest to see the woman when the body is bared.

Unlike the deacon the deaconess had no liturgical function and was expressly forbidden to go to the altar. According to the

Apostolic Constitutions she 'does not perform anything belonging to the office of presbyters or deacons, save only the keeping of the doors, and the ministering to the presbyters in the baptism of women, on account of decency'.

The structure that has now been described consisted then of bishops, priests and deacons, together with the five minor orders, an order of deaconesses and one of widows. Initially this was not a graded hierarchy, i.e. a series of offices through which an individual might advance from the bottom to the top. A deacon, for example, might remain a deacon all his life or he might become a bishop without the necessity of passing through the presbyterate. This was because the various orders were regarded as functions rather than as offices; for the harmonious conduct of the Church's life all were necessary, and one was not more important than another, since each was essential. Nor was there at first any rigid distinction between clergy and laity, for all belonged to the priesthood of the whole Body and each had his or her part to play, whether performing the function of a bishop or that of a simple member of the congregation. In time, however, the Church underwent a process of clericalization; function was displaced by position; the ministry was set over against the Church; the laity became more and more passive. The full results of this are not to be seen until the Middle Ages, but the beginnings of the development are already evident in the third century.

If, however, in its beginnings the Church was a growing structure rather than an organization, this did not mean that it failed either to order its activities or to regulate its life, and foremost amongst its arrangements was the development of the parochial system.

The word 'parish', which is the English equivalent of the Latin *paroecia* and the Greek *paroikia*, originally meant a community of foreigners or sojourners. Thus in all the large cities of the Roman empire there were to be found 'parishes' of Jews, i.e. communities of foreigners who were not citizens in the strict sense of the word. In the first centuries of its history, Christianity was largely a city religion and the Christian community in each centre was a 'parish'. 'Parish', therefore, referred to the community and not to the geographical area in which it lived, and this was a not inappropriate use of the term since, according to I Peter, Christians are 'sojourners and pilgrims', for, in the words of Hebrews, 'we have not here an abiding city, but we seek after the city which is to come'.

The leader and pastor of this community was the bishop who, as we have seen, was the chief liturgical minister and the one who was responsible for the care of the flock, beneath him being the other orders who acted in certain spheres as his delegates, while remaining always his subordinates. Even when the community became so large that it had to be divided into several groups, each being provided with its own building for worship, these groups were still regarded as part of the one community or parish over which the bishop presided. So Rome by the middle of the third century might be organized into several ecclesiastical regions and have as many as forty basilicas or church buildings but it was still one parish under one bishop.

The situation began to change when the Church gradually established itself in the countryside and new centres of worship were erected. The organization of these rural churches was not uniform throughout the empire. In North Africa a bishop of full rank was appointed wherever a Christian community existed. In Syria and parts of Asia Minor each country church was provided with a resident staff supervised by *chorepiscopoi* or itinerant bishops who were answerable to the bishop of the nearest large city. In the districts around Alexandria the villages were entrusted to presbyters under the superintendence of the bishop of Alexandria, and it was this practice that was most widespread in the West. There the country churches were at first in the nature of mission stations, centres of evangelism served by clergy sent out from the city, and they were still part of the one 'parish' or community under the bishop's rule. It was only in the sixth century, in Gaul in particular, that each was provided with its own resident staff of clergy.

Side by side with these were the oratories or chapels built on their estates by rich landowners for themselves, their tenants and their slaves. This was a practice which the Church encouraged and so we find, for example, John Chrysostom († 407) suggesting that where the cost was too great for one man to bear he should either seek the co-operation of his neighbours or build the church in sections, starting with the sanctuary, adding when possible and leaving it to his heirs to provide a porch or a forecourt. It is indeed from these estate oratories that the majority of parish churches today are descended, and we may note that of the thirty-seven churches in Auxerre in the sixth century, twenty-four were originally oratories and only six mission stations.

The main stages of the later development may now be indicated briefly. First the country churches which had been dependent for their finances upon the bishop received separate endowments, provided in many instances by the landowners who had erected them, and these same landowners reserved the right to nominate a priest, thus initiating the practice of private patronage. Second, under Charlemagne (768–814), a movement was set on foot to have a church and priest in every village. Third, decentralization began so that the bishop, while retaining the right to consecrate all churches, to ordain all clergy, to grant them permission to officiate, to confirm and to hold regular visitations, allowed a certain amount of local autonomy. Fourthly, even the city was split up into several districts with its own local ministry. Fifthly, each church was assigned a territorial district which it was to serve. At the same time a new terminology was gradually accepted with the adoption of the word diocese. This was used by the Romans to refer to certain civil divisions of the empire and was taken over by the Church to signify a district governed by a bishop. At first it was synonymous with parish, but eventually the latter term was applied to the area under the supervision of a priest, while diocese was used of the aggregate of these areas under a bishop, and province of those dioceses within the jurisdiction of an archbishop or metropolitan.

Three main features of Church organization, properly so-called, remain to be considered if this aspect of the picture of the Church's making is to be complete: these are the holding of councils, the growth of canon law and the development of the papal supremacy.

As a corporate Body there was need for the Church, represented by its leaders, to meet together from time to time to arrive at a common mind upon such questions as inevitably arose over matters of doctrine and discipline. This might be at what is now called the diocesan level, i.e. an assembly of the bishop and his presbyters, or at the provincial level, i.e. a synod of all the bishops of a province, or at the ecumenical level, i.e. a council of all the bishops of the Church. The example was set by the apostles themselves in holding a council at Jerusalem, described in Acts 15, to consider a dispute which had arisen in Antioch. So later we hear of synods in Asia Minor to deal with Montanism towards the end of the second century, of one at Iconium c. 230 to discuss heretical baptism, of one at Antioch in 269 to condemn Paul of Samosata, of one at Elvira c. 303 to regulate Christian life in a secular society and of one at Arles in 314 whither certain Western bishops were summoned by Constantine to review the claims of the schismatic Donatist group in North Africa. Nicaea however, which met in 325, was the first ecumenical council, and its inception would appear to have been due to the emperor himself, possibly under the influence of his adviser Hosius, bishop of Cordova. This council differed from its predecessors in three important particulars: it was convened by the emperor who had power both to compel attendance and to provide travelling facilities; it was an attempt for the first time to have represented all parts of the Church, and its decisions were eventually accepted as authoritative by the general body of Christians.

The number of these ecumenical or general councils is differently reckoned in different parts of Christendom today. The Church of England recognizes four—Nicaea in 325, Constantinople in 381, Ephesus in 431 and Chalcedon in 451. To these are sometimes added two more, the second (553) and third (680–1) of Constantinople, which only ratified the decisions of previous councils. The Eastern Church would add those of Nicaea in 787 and Constantinople in 879. The Roman Church would include many others, although Roman historians are not always consistent with one another.

Besides dealing with specific heresies, these councils promulgated a series of enactments to which the name 'canons' was given. A 'canon' meant originally a measuring rod or standard and was applied to the conciliar laws because they offered a standard of right conduct for Church members. As illustrative of the kind of law formulated, we may take several canons from the Council of Nicaea.

1. If anyone has been obliged to undergo a surgical operation from disease, or has been castrated by barbarians, let him continue in the clergy. But if anyone in good health has so mutilated himself, it is right that, if he be enrolled among the clergy, he should cease from his ministrations; and that from henceforth no such person should be promoted. As, however, it is plain that this is said with reference to those who dare to mutilate themselves, therefore, if

any persons have been so mutilated by barbarians, or by their own masters, and in other respects are found worthy, the canon allows them to be admitted to the clerical office.

17. Since many persons of the ecclesiastical order, being led away by covetousness, and a desire of filthy lucre, have forgotten the Holy Scripture which says, 'he gave not his money to usury', and in lending require the hundredth part, the holy and great Synod considers it right that if anyone after this decision shall be found receiving money for what he has advanced, or going about the business in any other way, as by requiring the whole and a half, or using any other device for filthy lucre's sake, he should be deposed from the clergy, and struck out of the list.

20. Since there are some persons who kneel on the Lord's Day and in the days of Pentecost; in order that all things may be observed in like manner in every parish, the holy Synod has decreed that all should at those times offer up their prayers to God standing.

It will be seen from this brief selection that these canons were concerned to govern the internal affairs of the Church and indeed the sum total of conciliar canons was held to make up a body of Church law which was known as Canon Law to distinguish it from the Roman Civil Law. In putting forward these enactments the Church was exercising its right to make rules and regulations for its members and was continuing the legislative authority which had been operative in the Old Israel and is a necessary element in any corporate life. In the fourth and fifth centuries the written law of the Church was by no means adequate to its needs, because, on the one hand, the Canon Law had been produced somewhat haphazardly to meet specific difficulties and abuses and, on the other hand, each province only accepted the canons of the general councils and those of its own local synods. In order therefore to provide the Church with a comprehensive system, collections of canons were made to guide a bishop when in difficulty as to the right course of action to take. Several of these collections were made in Rome at the end of the fifth and the beginning of the sixth century, of which that of Dionysius Exiguus was the most important—he was a Scythian monk living in Rome in the first decades of the sixth century. The *Dionysiana*, as it was known, was the first important attempt to provide the Church of the Western empire with a uniform system of law and it was followed by more private collections which culminated in the *Decretum* of Gratian in the twelfth century.

These collections included not only canons but also what were known as decretals, i.e. letters from the bishops of Rome answering questions referred to them for decision. A compendium of Forged Decretals, sometimes called *Pseudo-Isidore*, produced in France between 841 and 851, contributed greatly to the enhancement of papal authority in the Middle Ages, but even before this time the papacy had achieved a position of pre-eminence in the Western Church. How did this come about?

The primacy of Rome was at first the primacy of the local church, which itself rested upon three factors. Since it was the church of the imperial capital, its prestige was naturally great, so much so that when Ignatius of Antioch was taken under armed escort to Rome *c.* 114 he sent a letter on ahead to the Christian community asking them not to intercede with the government and thereby possibly rob him of the crown of martyrdom. To this influence must also be added a certain moral ascendancy to which Dionysius, bishop of Corinth, testifies in a letter to Soter, bishop of Rome, 175–182: 'This has been your practice from the beginning; to do good to all the brethren in various ways and to send supplies to many churches in every city.' The third factor was the close association of the city with the two apostles Peter and Paul, so that it was, if not of apostolic origin, at least of apostolic organization. It is not surprising therefore nor unfitting that the

Church of Rome should have had an acknowledged pre-eminence among other churches, and clear evidence of this is afforded by the Epistle of Clement to the Corinthians, written in the last quarter of the first century. A quarrel had apparently broken out at Corinth where the younger generation had set itself against the older and deprived the bishop and deacons of their functions. It is possible that they were motivated by the desire for a new distribution of positions of authority on the analogy of pagan religious organizations in which officers served for a short time and were then replaced. These facts became known at Rome and the faithful decided to intervene. Three men were despatched bearing a letter, written by Clement in the name of the church, reprimanding the Corinthians for their behaviour; the mission was evidently successful, as some seventy or so years later this epistle was still being read there in church.

A succession of Roman bishops, remarkable for their comprehensiveness, sense of order and moderation, further increased the reputation of the community in the capital city and with it their own fame too. The leader of such a church naturally in time received the respect initially given to the church as a whole and so the primacy of the Roman bishop was gradually accepted, and the third canon of the Council of Constantinople, 381, reads: 'The bishop of Constantinople shall have the primacy of honour next after the bishop of Rome, because that Constantinople is New Rome.' Yet, it will be noted, this is not a primacy of jurisdiction—to the establishment of this three further factors were at work: conciliar and imperial decisions; the efforts and claims of several outstanding popes and the pressure of political events.

In the year 343 a council met at Sardica and amongst its canons, promulgated to deal with certain situations arising out of the Arian controversy, were two which related to the right of a deposed bishop to seek a rehearing. It was enacted that the bishop of Rome should be consulted and should have the right to decide whether or not the case was to be reheard and, if so, by whom. So certain new but limited powers were conferred upon the pope by the action of this council. In the year 382 a council met at Rome to consider the case of Ursinus who had been Damasus' rival for the bishopric. This council presented a petition to the emperor Gratian who, in his reply, declared that (i) the bishops of those provinces under the direct metropolitan control of Rome were to be tried at Rome; (ii) other bishops were to be tried by the local metropolitan; (iii) in the case of metropolitans, they were to be tried either at Rome or by judges appointed by the bishop of Rome; (iv) ordinary bishops throughout the Western empire could appeal to the pope or to a synod of fifteen neighbouring bishops. This marks a great advance in the development of the papal jurisdiction through a direct grant of powers by the civil authority; in theory, if not yet in practice, the papal supremacy over the West had been largely asserted.

But the basis of papal supremacy, as it became accepted throughout the West up to the Reformation, was not just conciliar or civil; a more theological argument was also evolved. In this development Stephen (254–7) would appear to have been the prime mover. Taking his starting-point from the Petrine text, 'Thou art Peter, and upon this rock I will build my church' (Matt. 16. 18), Stephen argued that Peter was the leader of the apostles, that Peter was the first bishop of Rome and that he, Stephen, was therefore the successor of Peter and had authority over every other bishop. This thesis was neither readily nor immediately accepted by all, and in North Africa a council under Cyprian roundly asserted in 256 that 'no one of us setteth himself up as a bishop of bishops'. The claim, however, persisted and in 382 at a Roman council under Damasus it received its first official definition to the effect that the primacy of Rome was grounded on the promise of Christ to Peter. Since this depended not only on one interpretation of the Gospel text but also on the belief that Peter was the first bishop of Rome, a change was made in the episcopal lists. There are extant four early lists of the names of the bishops of Rome; those of Hegesippus, Irenaeus and Eusebius and that of Liberius. In the first three Peter and Paul appear in a class by themselves as the apostolic 'founders' of the church in Rome, and then the order of the bishops, from the first one Linus onwards, is recorded. In the fourth list, which emanated from Rome in 354, Paul has disappeared and Peter has become first bishop—so the facts of history were conveniently modified to support a favoured theory.

The Petrine claim was carried further by two other popes. Boniface I (418–22) received an appeal from the people of Corinth concerning the consecration of a certain Perigenes. Boniface replied in three letters, asserting that (i) the Roman see is the see of Peter and that Peter lives on in his see; (ii) 'this church is, as it were, a head over the members; and if anyone is separate from it he is an alien to the Christian religion, as having failed to remain in the body'; (iii) while 'bishops hold one and the same office', they should 'recognize those to whom for the sake of ecclesiastical discipline they are bound to be in subjection'.

Leo I (440–61) gave the theory its final form, claiming, in five sermons delivered to an audience of some two hundred bishops assembled to celebrate the anniversary of his consecration, that (i) Peter had supreme authority entrusted to him by Christ; (ii) Peter was the first bishop of Rome; (iii) Peter's authority has been perpetuated in his successors; (iv) the authority of other bishops is not derived immediately from Christ but mediately from Peter, and (v) while the authority of individual bishops is limited to their own dioceses, that of the bishop of Rome was over the whole Church of which he was the governor.

The acceptance of this authority was not a little due to contemporary political events. The fall of Rome in 410 and the consequent dissolution of the normal civil power left Innocent I (402–17) the leading personage in the imperial capital. His prestige—and he was a man of considerable capabilities—was great, and as province after province fell before the invaders, it was to him that people looked as the one stable figure of authority in an insecure world. It is not surprising therefore that his supremacy was generally acknowledged. By the time of Leo († 461) the political chaos was yet more advanced and even those parts of the Western Church, in particular North Africa, which had preserved their sturdy independence hitherto, were only too willing to avail themselves of his good offices and to subject themselves to his supreme jurisdiction. The East, still under imperial control and protection, was less ready to accept such a supremacy and gradually became more and more aloof from its Western counterpart.

It has been said with some cynicism but with some truth that the Roman Church was the ghost of the Roman empire sitting on the grave thereof; and indeed much of the prestige of the old civil power passed, at its defeat, to the bishop of Rome as the head of the Western Church throughout what are usually called the Dark Ages and the Middle Ages.

3

Church and State

ALTHOUGH the Church may be legitimately regarded as an organism, growing and developing according to its inner principle of life, no organism matures in a vacuum. The Church owed not a little to its environment and in particular to its relation to contemporary society and to the State. This relation changed in the course of the centuries from one of hostility to partnership and ultimately to something near domination, of the Church by the State (in the East), and of the State by the Church (in the West).

In the early days, after Pentecost, the Roman government took slight notice of the Church. Opposition came first from the Jews alone, and Gallio, proconsul of Achaia, typified the official attitude when, asked by the Jewish community at Corinth to condemn Paul, he replied: 'They are questions about words and names and your own law, look to it yourselves; I am not minded to be a judge of these matters.' To the Romans indeed Christianity was indistinguishable from the Judaism from which it had sprung; it was only gradually that the distinction between Church and Synagogue became too apparent to ignore, and until then Christianity enjoyed the toleration accorded its parent.

It was in the reign of Nero that the Church first added to its role of honour the names of those martyred by the State, and in this case there seems every reason to accept the statement of the Roman historian Tacitus that it was in order to find a scapegoat for the emperor's unprincipled action of setting fire to a quarter of Rome to clear space for his building programme.

But all human efforts, all the lavish gifts of the emperor, all the propitiations of the gods, did not banish the sinister belief that the conflagration was the result of an imperial order. Consequently, to get rid of the report, Nero fastened the guilt and inflicted the most exquisite tortures on a class hated for their abominations, called Christians by the populace. Christus, from whom the name had its origin, suffered the extreme penalty during the reign of Tiberius at the hands of one of our procurators, Pontius Pilate, and a most mischievous superstition thus checked for the moment, again broke out not only in Judaea, the first home of the evil, but even in Rome, where all things hideous and shameful from every part of the world find their centre and become popular. Accordingly, an arrest was first made of all who pleaded guilty; then, upon their information, an immense multitude was convicted, not so much of the crime of firing the city, as of hatred against mankind. Mockery of every sort was added to their deaths. Covered with the skins of beasts, they were torn by dogs and perished, or were nailed to crosses, or were doomed to the flames and burnt, to serve as nightly illumination when daylight had expired. Nero even offered his gardens for the spectacle, and was exhibiting a show in the circus, while he mingled with the people in the dress of a charioteer or stood aloft on a car. Hence, even for criminals who deserve extreme and exemplary punishment, there arose a feeling of compassion; for it was not, as it seemed, for the public good, but to glut one man's cruelty, that they were being destroyed.

In this first tragic encounter between Church and State the apostles Peter and Paul lost their lives, and henceforward persecution, or more precisely the danger of persecution, became a constant reality. Since the time of Augustine, it has become customary to speak of ten such persecutions, but this number is quite arbitrary and was probably chosen partly because of the ten plagues in Egypt and partly because of the ten kings who make war on the Lamb in the book of Revelation. There were not even six persecutions, the number adopted by Lactantius († *c.* 325), which prevailed throughout the whole empire. The persecutions were neither general nor continuous, so that the brethren in Gaul might be suffering indescribable tortures while those in Asia Minor were enjoying peace. What Eusebius wrote in reference to the reign of Trajan applies generally to every reign before the third century: 'Sometimes the people, sometimes the rulers in various places would lay plots against us, so that, although no great persecutions took place, local persecutions were nevertheless going on in particular provinces and many of the faithful endured martyrdom in various places.'

The juridical aspect of these persecutions is by no means clear. There is no certain evidence of any special legislative measures being enacted against Christians as such in the first two centuries. It would seem therefore that they were condemned as adherents of an illegal religion, illegal in the sense that it had not been licensed by law. Notice should also be taken of what is termed the provincial governors' *liberum arbitrium*, i.e. their discretionary powers as magistrates. In many instances it was the way in which they exercised these powers that made the difference between peace and oppression in any one area at any one time.

The causes of the persecutions were both general and particular. First among the general causes must be placed the attitude of the common people—popular opinion was against Christianity. This arose in part from ignorance: 'Men,' says Tertullian, 'give way to a dislike simply because they are entirely ignorant of the nature of the thing disliked.' It arose further from misrepresentation, so that garbled accounts of

Baptism, the Eucharist and the love-feasts or common meals gave currency to rumours of gross immorality. Hence according to the pagan in the *Octavius* of Minucius Felix (*c.* 200):

Now the story about the initiation of young novices is as much to be detested as it is well known. An infant, covered over with flour that it may deceive the unwary, is placed before him who is to be stained with their rites: this infant is slain by the young initiate with dark and secret wounds, who has been urged on as if to harmless blows on the surface of the flour. Thirstily—O horror!—they lick up its blood; eagerly they divide its limbs. By this victim they are pledged together; with this consciousness of wickedness they are pledged to mutual silence. Such sacred rites as these are more foul than any sacrileges. And of their banqueting it is well known that all men speak of it everywhere. On a solemn day they assemble at the feast, with all their children, sisters, mothers, people of every sex and of every age. There, after much feasting, when the fellowship has grown warm and the fervour of incestuous lust has grown hot with drunkenness, a dog that has been tied to the lampstand is provoked, by throwing a small piece of offal beyond the length of line by which it is attached, to jump forward; so the light being overturned and extinguished in the shameful darkness, the connections of abominable lust involve them in the uncertainty of fate.

This particularly unsavoury rumour was however not just hearsay; gatherings of this kind did indeed take place, but they were organized not by the faithful but by heretical groups which claimed the name of Christian. Outsiders, unable to distinguish between true and false believers, regarded all as tarred with the same brush. Of these lewd assemblies, as exemplified by a Gnostic sect known as the Carpocratians, Clement of Alexandria has preserved a description which is noticeably similar to the one that Octavius' pagan opponent has just given of what he mistakenly believed to be Christian gatherings:

These then are the doctrines of the excellent Carpocratians. These, so they say, and certain other enthusiasts for the same wickednesses, gather together for feasts (I would not call their meeting an Agape), men and women together. After they have sated their appetites ('on repletion Cypris, the goddess of love, enters', as it is said), then they overturn the lamps and so extinguish the light that the shame of their adulterous 'righteousness' is hidden, and they have intercourse where they will and with whom they will. After they have practised community of use in this love-feast, they demand by daylight of whatever women they wish that they will be obedient to the law of Carpocrates—it would not be right to say the law of God.

To immorality was added the charge of misanthropy. Christians formed a third race, neither Jew nor Gentile, which set itself apart from ordinary humanity and delighted in being a kill-joy. 'The world hates Christians,' according to the *Epistle of Diognetus* (c. 200), 'though not at all wronged, because they set themselves against its pleasures.' Moreover, to quote the *Octavius* again: 'You abstain from the pleasures of a gentleman; you never visit the shows, never join the processions, never attend the public banquets. You reject the sacred games and meat offered in sacrifice and libations poured out on the altars.' This last fact was accordingly interpreted as evidence that Christians were atheists who denied the existence of the gods and refused to offer sacrifices. This 'desperate and credulous faction', the Church, was therefore evidently the cause of every public disaster. 'If the Tiber rises as high as the city walls; if the Nile does not spread its waters over the fields; if the heavens give no rain; if there is an earthquake; if there is famine or pestilence, forthwith the cry resounds, "The Christians to the lion!"'

The government was not likely to have been unaffected by the uninformed prejudices of the majority, and moreover it had its own further reasons for opposition to the faith. There was first the refusal of Christians to take part in the worship of the emperor. This cult had begun with the apotheosis of Julius Caesar in 29 B.C., and had been encouraged by Domitian who even instructed his agents to issue his rescripts as from 'Our Lord and God'. Many Romans did not take the cult very seriously, but they nevertheless regarded it as a valuable means of securing unity amongst the numerous peoples that inhabited the empire; it provided a focus for their aspirations and to the enlightened was a useful political expedient if not spiritually beneficial. Between the worship of Caesar as Lord and that of Christ as Lord there were certain affinities which ultimately made them competitors. Both endeavoured to promote a universal religion; both believed in the incarnation of the divine in human form; both were of recent origin and had to contend not only with traditional cults but with each other; both claimed to confer similar benefits on mankind and so to deserve their allegiance. It was however the exclusivism of Christianity, with its refusal to worship any one other than Christ, be he emperor or not, that rendered a clash inevitable. Such conduct was regarded by the government as disloyal and treasonable, added to which Christians were known to be expecting a kingdom which would presumably supplant that of Rome. Even to Roman tolerance, in part compounded of indifference, there was a limit. The claim to be the one true faith for the whole world, the assertion that the genius of the emperor and the pagan gods were but demons, all this was regarded as a menace to stable civil government. Official policy therefore coincided with the popular viewpoint.

The situation, with Church confronting State, was therefore explosive and it only required some specific, even trivial, incident to produce a clash. These specific incidents make up the particular, as distinct from the general, causes of the persecutions. Evidence of them is however largely lacking, for the chroniclers were more concerned to describe the course and results of an outbreak of violence than to specify its genesis, but there are sufficient indications to provide some insight into the kind of motives that were at work. First among these is to be noted jealousy, of which there are at least three clear examples. In his *Second Apology* Justin Martyr has included the following interesting story:

A certain woman lived with an intemperate husband, she herself having been similarly intemperate. But when she came to the knowledge of the teachings of Christ she became self-controlled and tried to persuade her husband to be the same. But he continued in the same excesses and by his conduct alienated his wife from him. And she, thinking it wrong to live any longer as a wife with a husband who took every way of indulging in pleasure contrary to the laws of nature, and in violation of what is right, wished for a divorce. Her friends however persuaded her not to leave him on the grounds that eventually she might help him to amend. But when her husband went on a trip to Alexandria and was reported to be conducting himself worse than ever, in order that she might not continue to share his sins by remaining a companion of his table and bed, she gave him a bill of divorce and was separated. He immediately brought an accusation against her, alleging that she was a Christian. She however appealed to the emperor for time to arrange her affairs and as her husband could take no further, immediate steps against her, he turned on a certain Ptolemaeus, who was her teacher in the Christian doctrines. He persuaded a centurion who was a friend of his to ask Ptolemaeus one simple question: 'Are you a Christian?' When Ptolemaeus, who was a lover of truth and not at all disposed to be a deceiver, confessed that he was, he was thrown into prison. At last he was brought before the governor Urbicus who put to him the same question and upon his admission ordered him to be executed. As he was being led away, a certain Lucius, who was also a Christian, objected to the unreasonableness of the proceedings, only to be asked in his turn if he were of the faith. His affirmative reply issued in his immediate condemnation. And still a third having come forward, he too was condemned to be punished.

Justin Martyr himself was to suffer from similar motives. According to Eusebius his lectures on the Christian faith in Rome had met with considerable success to the annoyance of a Cynic philosopher, named Crescens, whom Justin had repeatedly overwhelmed in discussions before an audience. Crescens took the easy way of dealing with this by laying information against Justin as a Christian with the authorities. Similarly Apollonius (*c.* 180–5), a Christian of senatorial rank, was accused by someone unknown, who must obviously have been motivated by feelings of rivalry or jealousy. We can understand all the more readily therefore how Pliny, writing earlier in the century to Trajan, could record that a pamphlet had been published anonymously containing the names of a number of Christians and that others of the faithful had had their names 'given by an informer'.

Side by side with the activities of individuals must also be noted the part played by crowds. Mob violence is an ugly thing which can arise suddenly at moments of excitement and concentrate itself upon unsuspecting victims. Such seems to have been the case with Polycarp, bishop of Smyrna, who was martyred in 155 or 156. The occasion was the festival of the *Commune Asiae*, a notable anniversary of Caesar-worship of which Smyrna was one of the chief centres. There is good reason to suppose that the crowd, stirred by the ceremonies, turned against the Christians as known opponents of the imperial cult, and the Asiarch or High Priest, Philip, having tried in vain to persuade the bishop to acknowledge Caesar as Lord, condoned the action of the mob by ordering Polycarp's execution. A similar situation arose at Lyons and Vienne in 177 at the annual festival of the Three Gauls when sacrifices were offered to Rome and to the genius of the emperor. Christians, some betrayed by their own servants, were arraigned by the governor and were thrown to the wild beasts for the delectation of the crowd in the amphitheatre. According to the account of their sufferings, contained in a letter written shortly afterwards, the authorities were concerned 'to make of the faithful a spectacle, and to form a procession for the benefit of the crowds'.

To the jealousy of individuals and to mob violence must also be added the hostility of the Jews, whom Tertullian describes as 'fountains of persecution', and finally certain local conditions. An example of this last is to be seen in the persecution which broke out in Egypt and North Africa in the year 202. It can scarcely be coincidence that in the very year when the emperor Septimius Severus made public his adherence to the cult of Serapis a persecution should break out in those two areas which were its principal centres. This suggests that local adherents of Serapis, encouraged by the emperor's profession of belief and confident of his approval, seized the opportunity to strike a blow against their Christian rivals. The persecution under Maximinus (235–8), when Pontianus, bishop of Rome, and Hippolytus were banished to the mines of Sardinia—a verdict equivalent to the death sentence—was however less an attack upon Christianity as a deliberate reaction to the regime of his predecessor, Alexander Severus (222–35), who had included a statue of Jesus in his pantheon.

The third century A.D. saw something in the nature of a pagan religious revival which tended to increase opposition to the Church. The emperor Decius (249–51) was deeply affected by this movement and sought to remedy the growing weakness of the empire by a return to the old ways. To this end he determined to purify the Senate, to revive the office of censor, who had kept luxury within bounds, and to restore the ancient religion. The suppression of the Church followed logically from such a policy, for it had done much to foster disregard for the ancestral gods. The later persecutions, beginning with that of Decius, had therefore a cause additional to those previously listed and moreover the persecutions assumed a different character in so far as they no longer arose from sporadic local outbursts directed against individual Christians but were initiated by the emperors themselves against the Church and spread to all parts of their domain.

Early in 250 Decius issued his edict requiring all citizens to offer sacrifice, or at least incense and a libation; a certificate was then to be issued by the local commissioners declaring that its holder had complied with the order. As an example of these *libelli* we may quote one from Egypt:

To the commissioners in charge of the sacrifices in the village of Alexander's Isle, from Aurelius Diogenes, the son of Sabatus, of the village of Alexander's Isle, aged about 72, with a scar on his right eyebrow. I have always sacrificed to the gods, and now in your presence, according to the commands, I have sacrificed and made a libation and tasted of the victims; and I desire you to subscribe. Fare ye well. I, Aurelius Diogenes, have delivered this. I . . . X . . . saw him sacrifice and have subscribed. June 26, 250.

It is not surprising to find that many Christians gave way and these were divided into three groups: the *sacrificati*, i.e. those who had actually sacrificed; the *thurificati*, i.e. those who had burnt incense; and the *libellatici*, i.e. those who had obtained certificates by bribery. What to do with these people when, upon the death of Decius, peace was restored, was an acute problem for the Church—some were in favour of a policy of extreme rigour refusing to allow them readmittance at all; some were for lax measures permitting everyone who wished to re-enter without questions asked, while the leaders of the Church, including Cyprian in Carthage and Cornelius in Rome, were in favour of a midway position, tempering their disciplinary action to the degree of gravity of the offence.

The period of respite was however brief. Gallus (251–3), yielding to a sudden outbreak of popular animosity on the occasion of a plague which ravaged the empire towards the end of 252, gave orders that all should offer sacrifice to Apollo Salutaris for deliverance from pestilence. His successor Valerian (253–60) was more friendly disposed to the Church, but evil times fell on the empire in the form of attacks by frontier tribes and the way was paved for further denunciations of the Christians as a public danger. In August 257, under the influence of his minister Macrianus, a staunch adherent of the oriental cults, Valerian issued his first edict. This was concerned exclusively with the clergy who were commanded to sacrifice and to cease celebrating Christian worship. But the effect of this was only to turn the exiled bishops into missionaries without depriving them of their influence over their flocks at home and so a second edict was promulgated in 258 directing bishops, priests and deacons to be put to death; Christian matrons to be banished and members of the imperial household, who were or had been Christians, were to be sent to work in chains on the emperor's estates. The capture of Valerian by the Persian Shahpur I in 269 and his death shortly afterwards left his son Gallienus (270–80) as supreme ruler and he immediately put an end to the persecution by issuing rescripts which at last gave to Christianity the status of a legal religion.

For forty years the Church was free from State interference until towards the end of the reign of Diocletian (284–305). Like his predecessors Diocletian was concerned to restore the ancient glory of Rome. He therefore devised an entirely new scheme of government. There were to be two emperors who might reign for no longer than twenty years; there were also to be two Caesars to succeed their superiors should they die or resign. By this plan Diocletian aimed to secure the division of the cares of government without splitting the empire and a regular succession without the danger of a dynasty. It provided an opening for ambitious men who could become Caesars without engineering a revolution, and it had a religious basis in the worship of the gods. Diocletian did not at first appreciate that this last point necessarily involved the destruction of the Church, but under the influence of the Caesar Galerius, a fanatical pagan, and under pressure from the priests and philosophers he consented to the publication of his first edict on February 24th, 303. This ordered the demolition of churches, the burning of the Scriptures and the reduction to slavery of all the clergy. It did not directly sanction blood-shed, but it gave the opportunity since local officials were left free to treat those who refused to hand over the sacred books in any way they chose. A second edict commanded all the clergy to be imprisoned; a third all clergy to sacrifice on pain of torture, and a fourth, in 304, all laity to sacrifice or suffer for it.

In 305 Diocletian and Maximian abdicated, in accordance with the provisions of the new constitution, and this brought an end to the persecution in the West, although in the East, under Galerius, it continued for another six years. It was the triumph of Constantine at the Milvian Bridge, October 27th, 312, and the agreement between him and Licinius at Milan in the following year that saw the conclusion of hostility between the Church and the State which had persisted for so long a time.

The annals of the persecutions, consisting of the accounts of eye-witnesses, copies of the official transcriptions of the trials, etc., are both stirring and pitiful to read. While the fearlessness and endurance of the victims cannot but command admiration, the tortures to which they were submitted, either to persuade them to renounce Christ or to inflict on them a painful and slow death, were vicious and horrible. As a typical example of a cross-examination, we may take the record concerning Justin Martyr and his companions, who were executed in A.D. 163.

Rusticus, the prefect of Rome: Obey the gods at once, and submit to the Emperors.

Justin: To obey the commandments of our Saviour Jesus Christ is worthy neither of blame nor of condemnation.

Rusticus: What kind of doctrines do you profess?

Justin: I have endeavoured to learn all doctrines, but I have finally accepted the true doctrines, those namely of the Christians, even though they do not please those who hold false opinions.

Rusticus: Are those the doctrines that please you, you wretched fellow?

Justin: Yes, since I adhere to them with right dogma.

Rusticus: What is the dogma?

Justin: That according to which we worship the God of the Christians, whom we reckon to be one from the beginning, the maker and fashioner of the whole of creation, visible and invisible; and the Lord Jesus Christ, the Son of God, who had also been preached beforehand by the prophets as about to come to the human race, the herald of salvation and the teacher of good men.

Rusticus: Where do you assemble?

Justin: Where each one chooses and can; for do you fancy that we all meet in the very same place? No indeed, for the God of the Christians is not confined by space, but being invisible fills heaven and earth, and is everywhere worshipped and glorified by the faithful.

Rusticus: Tell me where you assemble or in what place you collect your followers.

Justin: I live above one Martin, at the Trinothinian Bath; and though I am now living in Rome for the second time, I know of no other meeting than his. And if anyone has wished to approach me, I have communicated to him the doctrines of truth.

Rusticus: Are you not then a Christian?

Justin: Yes, I am a Christian.

Rusticus: Tell me further, Chariton, are you also a Christian?

Chariton: I am a Christian by the command of God.

Rusticus: And what are you?

Euelpistus: A servant of Caesar. I too am a Christian, having been freed by Christ; and by the grace of Christ I partake of the same hope.

Rusticus: And you, are you a Christian?

Hierax: Yes I am a Christian, for I revere and worship the same God.

Rusticus: Did Justin make you Christians?

Hierax: I was a Christian and will remain one.

Paeon: I too am a Christian.

Rusticus: Who taught you?

Paeon: From our parents we received this good confession.

Euelpistus: I willingly heard the words of Justin, but from my parents also I learned to be a Christian.

Rusticus: Where are your parents?

Euelpistus: In Cappadocia.

Rusticus: Where are your parents?

Hierax: Christ is our true father, and faith in him is our mother; and my earthly parents are dead. When I was driven from Iconium in Phrygia, I came here.

Rusticus: And what have you to say? Are you also a Christian?

Liberianus: I too am a Christian, for I worship and reverence the only true God.

Rusticus: Listen, you who are called learned and think that you know true doctrines; if you are scourged and beheaded, do you believe you will ascend into heaven?

Justin: I hope that if I endure these things I shall have his gifts. For I know that to all who have thus lived there abides the divine favour until the consummation of the world.

Rusticus: Do you suppose then that you will ascend into heaven to receive some recompense?

Justin: I do not suppose it, but I know and am fully persuaded of it.

Rusticus: Let us then come now to the matter in hand, and which presses. Having come together, offer sacrifice to the gods.

Justin: No right-thinking man falls away from piety to impiety.

Rusticus: Unless you obey, you shall be mercilessly punished.

Justin: Through prayer we can be saved on account of our Lord Jesus Christ, even when we have been punished, because this shall become to us salvation and confidence at the more fearful and universal judgement seat of our Lord and Saviour.

The Others: Do what you will, for we are Christians, and do not sacrifice to idols.

Rusticus: Let those who have refused to sacrifice to the gods, and to yield to the command of the emperor be scourged, and led away to suffer the punishment of decapitation, according to the laws.

Justin and his companions were fortunate in that they had to endure no more than flogging and were then speedily despatched by beheading. Most other martyrs received harsher treatment. So Blandina, the slave girl, arrested at Lyons in 177, after torture and the running of the gauntlet in the amphitheatre, was first suspended on a cross and exposed to wild animals, then seated in a red-hot chair known as the frying-pan, and finally was trussed in a basket to be tossed by a bull before being stabbed to death. The records are indeed full of violence and brutality—of virgins violated, of old men thrown from their bedroom windows, of matrons dragged by the hair through the streets. Yet, in Tertullian's words, 'the blood of martyrs is the seed of the Church', and while some could not face the ordeal, the majority remained steadfast. When Constantine brought peace he was, among other things, only recognizing an obvious fact—the policy of suppression had failed; the Church had continued to grow from strength to strength, and since it seemed impossible to destroy it, it had to be reckoned with as a great power within the empire.

The new-won freedom and the victories of Constantine which had led to it seemed to many in the Church a clear indication of the workings of divine providence. The emperor's triumph could only have been due to God, and so Eusebius was prepared to hail Constantine as a new David with the empire as the Messianic Kingdom and the church of the Holy Sepulchre as the New Jerusalem. The kingdoms of this world had become the Kingdom of God and his Christ. As the God-given ruler, as the divine representative, Constantine's authority could not be limited to secular affairs alone. The government and welfare of mankind was his concern under God and this universal authority was presumed to extend to the Church as to the State. Moreover, if the result of the Milan declaration had been toleration, this did not mean religious neutrality on the part of the State, for an official cult was a feature of the unquestioned norm, and so when Constantine became a Christian, Christianity fast acquired the status of the official religion. Consequently, just as previously the pagan emperors, in their capacity of pontifex maximus, had regarded religion as an affair of State, so Constantine, by his very position and the tradition to which he was heir, was involved in the affairs of the Church. Such guidance as the Bible was able to give seemed to point in this same direction, for according to the New Testament secular authority is of divine institution, part of the natural moral order appointed by God, while in the Old Testament the king is as much a religious as a political figure, closely associated with all matters relating to the divine.

We therefore find the emperor seeking to further the cause of Christianity, on the negative side by prohibiting magic and private divination and closing temples known to be centres of immoral cults, and on the positive side by gifts of land and buildings to the Church. There is no reason to suppose that this was not in part prompted by his new religious faith, but in this instance religious faith coincided with political expediency, for Constantine saw in Christianity a means of securing the unity of the empire. It was to be expected therefore that if anything happened to disturb that unity he would act to preserve it. We see this in the case of the Donatists, a rigourist group in North Africa, who had cut themselves off from the main body because of its lenient treatment of the lapsed. We see it also in the emperor's decision to intervene in the Arian controversy and to summon the Council of Nicaea. The Church was quite content that he should do these things, and it approved too of his enforcement of conciliar canons and of his deportation of recalcitrant bishops deposed from their sees. The unity of Church and State was indeed very close, and under Constantine there is little hint of a dualist theory.

When in 340 the empire was divided between Constantine's two sons, Constans ruling the West and Constantius the East, the same relationship continued as under their father. It was however a somewhat anomalous situation. Constans was a supporter of the Nicene orthodoxy, as were the majority of Western Christians who were therefore quite willing to accept his championship, such as the arranging of the Council of Sardica in 343. Constantius was more favourably disposed to the Arian cause, as were the majority of Eastern Christians, partly through conservatism, partly through a failure to understand clearly the issues involved, and they were quite willing that he should continue his authority over the Church. When Constantius became sole emperor, upon the death of his brother in 350, his Western subjects were less happy about his position and those of the Easterns who rallied round Athanasius in his defence of Nicaea were equally unable to accept his right to determine matters of doctrine. Hence pressure of contemporary circumstances led to a changed conception of the Church-State relationship which found its clearest expression in a letter from Hosius of Cordova to

Constantius when the latter ordered him in 355 to excommunicate Athanasius and enter into communion with the Arians:

Intrude not yourself into ecclesiastical matters, neither give commands unto us concerning them; but learn them from us. God has put into your hands the kingdom; to us he has entrusted the affairs of the Church; and, as he who should steal the empire from you would resist the ordinance of God, so likewise fear on your part lest, by taking upon yourself the government of the Church, you become guilty of a great offence. It is written, 'Render unto Caesar the things that are Caesar's, and unto God the things that are God's.' Neither, therefore, is it permitted to us to exercise an earthly rule; nor have you, Sire, any authority to burn incense.

Hosius thus propounds the theory that the emperor is, under God, responsible for secular affairs and the bishop for Church matters. The dualist theory is here plainly enunciated to the effect that there are two distinct spheres, Church and State, which, while both responsible to God, are separate the one from the other. Thus Constantius' support for the Arian position led to a growing demand for ecclesiastical autonomy, and Athanasius could demand, with slight recollection of recent history: 'When did a judgment of the Church receive its validity from the emperor, or when was his decree ever recognized by the Church? There have been many councils and many judgements passed by the Church; but the fathers never sought the consent of the emperor thereto, nor did the emperor busy himself with the affairs of the Church.'

This dualism may be illustrated further from the Priscillianite controversy. Priscillian was a Spanish cleric whose teaching, as far as can be gathered from the very few documents that survive, was a compound of extreme asceticism with certain heterodox views concerning the Trinity and the Person of Christ. He was condemned, if not by name at least by implication, by a council at Saragossa in 380. This however did not deter the increasing number of his followers who had him consecrated bishop of Avila. His opponents, led by Ithacius of Ossonuba, appealed to the emperor Gratian who issued a rescript against 'pretended-bishops and Manichaeans'. Whereupon Priscillian made his way to Italy and through a friend at court succeeded in having it repealed. This acquittal involved the guilt of his accusers, for the official view was that they had been 'disturbers of the peace of the churches', and so Ithacius, to avoid arrest, fled to Gaul. The situation now changed through the murder of Gratian and the accession in 383 of Maximus to whom Ithacius appealed, charging Priscillian with Manichaeism and the practice of magic. A synod then met at Bordeau in 384, but Priscillian refused to acknowledge its authority and appealed to the emperor. The following year he was brought to trial at Trier, found guilty of magic and executed. Although the charge was a civil one, it was apparent to all that he had actually been condemned for heresy.

The close relationship of Church and State is evident throughout this series of events, but opposition to the whole proceedings, on dualist grounds, was voiced by Martin of Tours. He happened to be at the imperial court at Trier when Ithacius made his accusations, and he sought to dissuade the Spanish bishop from proceeding with the charges. When Ithacius refused to give way, Martin approached Maximus and extracted a promise that no blood would be shed, arguing that secular judges should not try ecclesiastical causes. It was sufficient for a heretic, upon condemnation by the Church, to be deprived of his see. Martin then left the court, only to return when he had learnt of what had taken place and of Maximus' decision to send a commission to Spain to round up Priscillian's followers. Martin refused to communicate with the blood-guilty Ithacians, but at last consented to do so when Maximus undertook to countermand his commission. In these events we see the precedent set for the later handing over of heretics to be executed by the secular power and the opposing viewpoint of Martin that Church and State should occupy themselves with their own affairs.

Yet this dualism, while commendable in its simplicity and certainly applicable where a pagan State and the Christian Church are in opposition, is scarcely adequate where there is a Christian ruler. In such circumstances the lines of demarcation become blurred and this was especially so in the fourth century when, as we have seen, the bishops themselves exercised civil jurisdiction. Moreover insofar as the ruler was a member of the Church, he was subject to its discipline and to moral censure should he default in his conduct. Considerations such as these led in the first instance to the reproving of the emperor for acting wrongly in the sight of God and ultimately to the claim that the civil power should be under ecclesiastical control. This is exemplified in the relations of Ambrose of Milan with the emperor Theodosius.

In 388 the Christians of Callinicum, a small town on the Euphrates, had burnt down a Jewish synagogue and some monks had also set fire to a church belonging to a group of Valentinian Gnostics. Theodosius ordered the local bishop to rebuild the synagogue at his own expense and the monks to be punished for their disorderly conduct. Ambrose however saw fit to intervene, arguing that this was in effect a condemnation of the bishop to martyrdom, since this was the only way he could avoid the apostasy he would certainly commit were he to obey the imperial command. Theodosius thereupon directed that the State should bear the cost of rebuilding the synagogue, but Ambrose was still not satisfied. He declared that in a Christian State no public money should be spent on non-Christian worship, and as for the plea that the State must maintain public order, religion was more important than

order. This was followed by a sermon from Ambrose specifically aimed at the emperor who was present in the congregation,
and indeed he went so far as to intimate that he would not
allow him to participate in the eucharistic offering if he did not
withdraw his decision. The emperor gave way. The importance
of this incident lies in the fact that in a matter of illegal
behaviour the Church had prevailed against the civil authority,
thus paving the way for the mediaeval debate between empire
and papacy which culminated in the humiliation of Henry IV
before Gregory VII at Canossa in 1070 and the declaration of
Innocent III that 'kings rule over their respective territories,
but Peter rules over the whole earth'.

The second incident relates to the rising of the populace at
Thessalonica in 390. One of the charioteers had been thrown
into prison on the charge of gross immorality, whereupon the
mob stormed the building, murdered the commander with
several of his staff and released their idol. Theodosius sent
secret orders for a massacre; soldiers were to surround the
amphitheatre when the people had gathered to see the games
and were then to slaughter the spectators. Although the
emperor relented and sent a revocation of his order, it arrived
too late and seven thousand were butchered. Ambrose accordingly excommunicated him and it was only after several
months and a public penance that Theodosius was restored to
communion on Christmas Day. So the Church had acted in a
case in which it was not directly involved and yet a further
step had been taken towards the mediaeval conflict when the
pope claimed the right to depose emperors.

The relation of Church and State is not one that is easily
settled and it is largely determined by the concrete historical
situation in which each finds itself. If hostility and persecution
is not to be condoned, dualism is not without its difficulties,
for while it rightly affirms that the State is not omnipotent, it
is hard to be precise as to what exactly belongs to each sphere,

and it involves the danger that part of life will be regarded as outside God's concern. In the East the harmony of Church and State prevailed; in the West, due to the barbarian invasions, the idea of a State-Church developed, but the rise of the papacy as the focus of supernational unity encouraged the idea of the ascendancy of the Church with its attendant clericalism. In this respect the Church was not only in the making in the early centuries, it is always in the making, and Church-State relations must inevitably remain fluid.

4

The Unity of the Church

IF CONSTANTINE'S concern for the unity of the Church, as noted in the last chapter, was based largely upon political considerations, the Church's own concern for its unity was not determined by any such argument from expediency. The Church was one and had to be one, not so that it might present a united front to the pagan world, but because that was the intention of its Founder and Lord. Jesus' prayer to the Father, as reported in the Fourth Gospel, was 'that they may be one, even as we are . . . that they may all be one; even as thou, Father, art in me, and I in thee, that they also may be in us'. Hence, according to the Epistle to the Ephesians, 'there is one body, and one Spirit, even as also ye were called in one hope of your calling; one Lord, one faith, one baptism, one God and Father of all'. So too Paul, hearing of divisions or schisms at Corinth, could ask, with the certainty that the reply would be negative, 'Is Christ divided?'

The oneness of the Church and the consequent scandal and even blasphemous crime of division were insisted upon again and again. To Cyprian, 'he who breaks the peace and concord of Christ, does so in opposition to Christ; he who gathers elsewhere than in the Church, scatters the Church of Christ'. 'Nothing angers God so much as the division of the Church,' declares Chrysostom; 'even if we have done ten thousand good deeds, those of us who cut up the fulness of the Church will be punished no less than those who cut his body.'

Believing that the oneness of the Church is the oneness of Christ in the unity of the Spirit, the Fathers were agreed that there could be no internal division. Of any two groups in opposition, one was the Church, the other was not. 'God is one, and Christ is one, and his Church is one, and the faith is one, and the people is one, in a substantial unity of body by the cement of concord. Unity cannot be severed'—so Cyprian formulated the principle accepted by all; the only problem was to decide which was the true Church. This was further complicated by the tendency to identify schism with heresy. One and the same writer can refer to a movement as both a schism and a heresy, but the general distinction was that schism was orthodox and involved the hiving off from the Church of a splinter group. So, according to Athanasius, heretics slay the word, whilst schismatics rend the seamless robe of Christ. Yet the facts were on occasion more stubborn than the theory that was applied to them allowed. This may be illustrated from the first important schism which centred in the Quartodeciman controversy.

It was apparently the custom of the churches in Asia Minor to commemorate Easter on the same day as the Jewish Passover, i.e. the 14th Nisan, whatever the day of the week, whereas other churches celebrated it on the Sunday following the 14th Nisan. This divergence of practice meant that one part of the Church was still fasting while another was feasting. This in itself however need not have given rise to friction had there not been resident in Rome a large community of Asiatics who insisted on observing the practice to which they had been accustomed. In A.D. 154–5 Polycarp, bishop of Smyrna, visited the capital to discuss the matter with Anicetus; each failed to convince the other and they agreed to differ. So the matter seems to have rested for some thirty-five years until *c*. 190 when Victor of Rome made an energetic attempt to secure uniformity. He held a synod and sent out requests for others to meet. The majority shared his view, but the synod of Asia under the leadership of Polycrates of Ephesus refused to conform, whereupon Victor cut the province off from communion with the church of Rome. His action called forth severe censure from many bishops, including Irenaeus of Lyons, and it seems to have had little effect. The question of the unity of the Church was not specifically posed, but the facts as recorded would have made it difficult for either side to substantiate a claim to be the true Church. The situation was further complicated by a charge of heresy, and while the Asian churches as a whole seem to have been entirely free from the taint, Blastus, who was active in Rome either shortly before or during the episcopate of Victor, apparently insisted not only upon the Quartodeciman dating but also on actually eating the Paschal lamb, and was therefore regarded as wanting to introduce Judaism secretly. Schism and heresy thus tended to merge.

Asia also figures in the next schism which equally shaded over into heresy. This was the movement of which Montanus was the founder. This man, who first attracted notice in either A.D. 156 or 172, was a native of the village of Ardabau on the borders of Phrygia and is said to have been a convert from paganism, having previously occupied the position of a priest of the cult of Cybele. If this indeed be true, then he seems to have transferred from that worship the fervid and ecstatic spirit that it nurtured, since he became famous for his transports in which he uttered strange sayings and was consequently regarded as a prophet. With him were soon associated two women, Maximilla and Priscilla, to whom similar authority was ascribed.

At first this 'revivalist' movement seems to have been

essentially orthodox and was in the main a reaction to Gnosticism. This latter, in its Christian dress, was undeniably a heresy, being a compound of Hellenistic, Oriental and unorthodox Jewish ideas and constituting, in its developed forms as propounded by Valentinus and Basilides, a kind of second-century theosophy. Common to all its types was the rejection of the Old Testament, on the grounds that it was the record of an inferior deity, the demiurge, from whom man was set free by the Supreme God revealed for the first time by Jesus Christ; the affirmation that matter is evil and that consequently the humanity of Christ was not real but only a semblance, and the rejection of any kind of eschatological expectation. The Montanists on the other hand upheld the authority of the Old Testament, opposed the Gnostic docetism and expected a speedy end of the present age when the heavenly Jerusalem would descend at Pepuza, the home of Priscilla. The followers of Montanus were also remarkable for their extreme asceticism which revealed itself in their emphasis on celibacy, their condemnation of second marriages and their prescription of long and severe fasts. Their leaders claimed to be speaking under the direct inspiration of the Spirit who had now been poured out in fulfilment of Jesus' promise at the Last Supper to send the Paraclete or Comforter.

The moral earnestness of the Montanists, their essential orthodoxy, and the authority with which they spoke in its support as mouthpieces of the Spirit were not unattractive. Irenaeus brought to Rome a letter from the bishops of Gaul suggesting conciliatory treatment of them; Tertullian in Africa went over to them, and Zephyrinus, Victor's successor at Rome, seems to have been on the verge of approving them —yet condemnation, not only as a schism but as a heresy, was their eventual lot. They were opposed on various grounds: first, as arrogant for claiming to supersede the revelation contained in the apostolic writings; second, as extravagant in their doctrine of the Spirit who, to the orthodox, had been present in the Church since the day of Pentecost when Jesus' promise had been fulfilled; third, as disruptive and therefore as dangerous at a time when the Church was menaced by the State from without and by Gnosticism from within; and finally as rebellious insofar as they refused to accept the rulings of the bishops who were regarded as the guardians of the Church's unity and faith. This rejection of existing authority reveals their schismatic character, and soon they were being charged with heresy, although at the outset such a charge was hardly justified. Bishops condemned them, synods formulated canons against them, yet they managed to survive in isolated groups for some two hundred years.

The motivation of the two schisms at which we have so far glanced is relatively easy to determine—Quartodecimanism having arisen from the coexistence of two separate traditions which naturally conflicted with a desire for uniformity, and Montanism being a reaction by a puritanical group, determined to have no compromise with worldly standards, against a heresy which tended, in some of its manifestations, to undermine Christian moral conduct and to deny the truth of the Gospel. In later schisms personal ambitions and antipathies, economic considerations and even national aspirations were to play their part, and the situation was aggravated by the conduct of the State authorities.

In A.D. 250 the emperor Decius issued an edict requiring all citizens throughout the empire to offer a sacrifice of homage. Those who refused were to be tortured, and if they persisted were to be exiled or executed. Many Christians were unable to withstand this test of their faith, and the apostates were numerous. Many, according to Cyprian:

did not wait to be apprehended . . . many were conquered before the battle and prostrated before the attack. Nor did they even leave it to be said for them that they seemed to sacrifice to idols unwillingly. They ran to the market place of their own accord; freely they hastened to spiritual death, as if they had formerly wished it, as if they would embrace an opportunity now provided which they had always desired.

When the death of Decius eventually brought peace, the Church was faced with a disciplinary problem of considerable magnitude: what was to be done with the backsliders? Three courses were possible: the punishment could be made to fit the crime, i.e. there could be a graded series of penalties or penances dependent upon the gravity of the apostasy; the punishment could be remitted entirely, i.e. no disciplinary action of any kind need be taken; the punishment could be made absolute, i.e. no apostate should be allowed readmittance to the Church. Schism took place when three separate groups each adopted one of these three attitudes.

The first represents the policy of Cyprian, who had been made bishop of Carthage very shortly after his conversion to Christianity and whose election had been opposed by a group of presbyters jealous at his speedy advancement. He had gone into hiding during the persecution, believing that such an action would better serve the interests of his flock than martyrdom, and had postponed any decision on the matter until a council could be summoned. This met in the spring of 251 and decided that those who had sacrificed were to do penance and only be reconciled at the point of death; that those who had obtained forged certificates saying they had sacrificed were to do penance for a shorter or longer period and then be reconciled; and that those who had entertained the idea of apostasy were to confess and undergo whatever suitable penance was imposed. Cyprian's opponents, led by a presbyter Novatus and a deacon Felicissimus, supported a much more lenient policy, refused to communicate with those who accepted Cyprian and induced two heretical and three lapsed bishops to consecrate a certain Fortunatus as their leader.

While this schism was developing in Carthage, another broke out in Rome. There, after the execution of Fabian on January 20th, 250, there had been an interregnum for over fifteen months as the persecution was too severe to enable a successor to be appointed. But in March 251 Cornelius became bishop, only to be opposed immediately by Novatian, one of the leading presbyters and a man renowned for his learning which he had crystallized in a treatise on the Trinity. Novatian seems to have been influenced partly by personal disappointment at not being elected himself but more by his extreme rigorist views and a zeal for strict discipline—he would allow no reconciliation of the apostates. He managed to obtain consecration and set himself up as rival bishop to Cornelius.

The situation now became more confused since Fortunatus sent envoys to Rome and Novatian despatched representatives to Carthage where there were soon three claiming to be bishop—Cyprian, the lax Fortunatus and the strict Maximus who was a Novatianist. Novatianism spread with some rapidity, gaining a foothold in Gaul and Spain and especially in Asia Minor where it persisted until the sixth century. But the wisdom of the Church's concern for the lapsed and its refusal to deny hope to the repentant sinner gradually prevailed and Novatianism did not seriously imperil its unity; it did however lead directly to a near schism.

Certain of the followers of Novatian, baptized in schism, desired to return to the Church and the question was therefore raised as to whether or not their baptism should be recognized. The Roman and African churches held opposite points of view. In Rome their baptism was deemed valid but in need of completion by the laying on of hands. In Carthage their baptism was deemed to be no baptism and, therefore, the whole initiation rite, including water and the laying on of hands, was necessary. Cyprian held three councils on this subject: one in 255, another before Easter 256, and the last on September 1st, 256. Of this last we have a very interesting account in a document recording the actual words used by the eighty-seven bishops of Africa, Numidia and Mauretania who were present. The *Acta* open with an allocution of Cyprian who, after reading the letter of a Mauretanian bishop Jubianus together with his own reply, continued:

It remains for us to express our opinions one by one, without claiming to judge anyone or to excommunicate those who may not agree with our view. For no one among us sets himself up as a bishop of bishops, no one tyrannizes over his colleagues, nor terrorizes them in order to compel their assent, seeing that every bishop is free to exercise his power as he thinks best.

Each bishop then delivered his opinion, the verdicts being unanimously in favour of Cyprian's view of the necessity of rebaptism. The African delegates who carried these decisions to Rome were not only not received but were left without any lodging, and Stephen, the new bishop, wrote to his adherents in Africa denouncing Cyprian as a 'false Christ, a false apostle, and a dishonest worker'. Whereupon Cyprian sought the support of the church of Asia Minor which shared his view and wrote to Firmilian of Caesarea. It was in vain that Dionysius of Alexandria sought to play the role of peacemaker, but a solution was at hand, due to the pressure of secular politics. The emperor Valerian promulgated an edict against the Christians and Stephen died a martyr's death on August 2nd, 256, as Cyprian himself was to do four years later on September 14th. By the removal of the principal actors from the scene a complete schism was thus avoided.

If State intervention prevented an open schism in this instance, it sparked off yet another and more serious division in Africa some fifty years later and this was to last until the complete disappearance of the faith in the attacks of the Saracens. Just as Novatianism was part of the aftermath of the Decian persecution, so Donatism stemmed from that inaugurated by Diocletian. His rescript of February 24th, 303, required the handing over by the Christians of their Scriptures to be burned. Some complied quite eagerly, even throwing the books into the flames themselves; others prevaricated, handing over either heretical works—such was the case with Mensurius, bishop of Carthage—or only part of their library.

The rigorist attitude to such conduct was to condemn it as apostasy and to affirm that the *traditores* or handers-over could no longer be regarded as members of the Church nor, if they were clergy, as having any right to exercise their former authority. This was first given expression at a small council of Numidian bishops who met at Cirta under the presidency of Secundus of Tigisis to consecrate a certain Silvanus. Secundus opened the proceedings by enquiring into the fitness of the assembled bishops, six of whom were charged as *traditores* and four of these confessed their guilt. One of the acccused however, Purpurius of Limata, counter-attacked with a similar charge against the president and threatened to murder anyone who might oppose him. It was deemed politic to pursue the matter no further, and Silvanus, despite the protests of the local church of Cirta, was duly consecrated. Nevertheless sufficient had been said to make it plain that the question of *traditor*-bishops was likely to be a difficult one and matters came to a head with the death of Mensurius in 311.

Caecilian, Mensurius' leading deacon, was consecrated as his successor but immediately ran into opposition. The rigorists regarded him with disfavour both because he had supported Mensurius in a lenient policy towards the lapsed and because he was suspected of being unsympathetic, not so say harsh, in his treatment of certain confessors and martyrs. They therefore invited Secundus to intervene and he came post-haste to Carthage with seventy Numidian bishops. They condemned Caecilian on the grounds that he had been conse-crated by a *traditor*, one Felix of Aptunga, and they proceeded to elect a reader, Majorinus, in his stead. They then sent embassies announcing Majorinus' consecration to Rome, Spain and Gaul and letters reporting their decisions to the African provinces. So the schism was inaugurated, Majorinus being soon succeeded by Donatus from whom the sect took its name.

The next stage in the controversy began with the emperor's action, as patron and not as persecutor. Constantine ordered the restoration of all churches and lands that had been recently confiscated and declared the clergy exempt from municipal levies. This was applied only to Caecilian and those in com-munion with him. The Donatists had no alternative than to appeal against this and asked that some Gallican bishops, who might be presumed to be neutral, should consider the matter. The synod met in Rome in October 313 and pronounced in favour of Caecilian. The Donatists were naturally not satisfied and again appealed to the emperor who, with some annoyance, summoned a council to meet at Arles in 314. Caecilian was again vindicated and canons were passed condemning the Donatist practice of rebaptism and declaring that ordination by a *traditor*-bishop was valid. After some delay an enquiry was conducted in Africa into the case of Felix of Aptunga who was found innocent of *traditio*, it being disclosed that the evidence against him rested on forged letters. Again the Donatists appealed, this time to the emperor in person; again Caecilian was acquitted and this was followed in 317 by a law exiling the Donatist leaders and confiscating their churches—an action that rallied the nationalists of Numidia to their side as opponents of the hated occupying Roman power. Caecilian determined to enforce this law; soldiers were put at his disposal, massacres followed and the division of African Christianity into two rival Churches became permanent, despite the demonstration in 320 that Silvanus of Cirta had himself been a *traditor*, thus compromising the whole Donatist position.

Nor was the situation eased by the tolerance granted in 321; this only provided the occasion for Donatism to grow from strength to strength so that by the middle of the fourth century it numbered as many as three hundred bishops. Such indeed was its ascendancy that in 346 Donatus felt himself strong enough to approach the emperor Constans with a view to his being recognized as sole bishop of Carthage. Two envoys, Paul and Macarius, were sent to Africa but they were so anti-Donatist in their sympathies that when they sought to penetrate into Numidia they were met with such hostility that they had to call troops to their aid. Force was met with force, and Donatus of Bagai summoned the Circumcellions to the attack.

These Circumcellions, who were so named because they dwelt 'around the shrines' (*circum cellas*) living off the gifts of the worshippers, were peasants actuated by religious zeal and economic grievances. Wielding their clubs or 'Israels', they terrorized the countryside and were alternately favoured and disfavoured by the Donatist leaders depending upon the latter's need of their armed support. The battle with Macarius and his men went against them and the outcome was a severe repression of Donatism which only came to an end with the accession of Julian in 361 and his recalling of all exiled Christians.

In Africa this edict had the effect desired by the emperor; strife immediately broke out and the Donatists rose to power again on a wave of popular religious fury. Their new leader

Parmenian was opposed to violence, moderate in his views and not without intellectual ability which he demonstrated in a work defending the claims of his Church, a work of which fragments only remain, in the reply by the Catholic Optatus of Milevis. Violence however broke out once more in 372 when Firmus, a chieftain of the Jubaleni clan, led a revolt against the imperial authorities and received the support of the Donatists who experienced further repressive measures when the rebellion was crushed three years later. Yet they soon managed to reassert themselves and for the rest of Parmenian's episcopate, until 391, they maintained their predominance. So secure did they feel, that they could even indulge in internal schisms—the Maximianists opposing Primian, Parmenian's successor at Carthage—and then, through the prompting and example of Optatus of Thamugadi they gave support to yet another anti-Roman revolt led by Gildo, a younger brother of Firmus. The Donatists did not fare so well after the overthrow of Gildo in 398 as they had done after the suppression of Firmus, and indeed the next twelve years witnessed their eclipse. The State, more and more menaced by the invasions of the Germanic tribes, determined to have no further truck with a movement whose loyalty was suspect and the Catholics launched an energetic counter-attack under the competent direction of Aurelius of Carthage and Augustine of Hippo.

To each Donatist stronghold an able Catholic opponent was consecrated and they availed themselves of imperial legislation to crush them wherever possible. Their efforts were backed by a series of councils and by a voluminous literary offensive in which Augustine played a major role. At first the Donatists gave as good as they received and Petilian of Constantine wrote forcibly in their defence. The situation however steadily deteriorated, violence becoming widespread until the Catholics determined on open persecution. In 405 the emperor Honorius pronounced the Donatists to be heretics and their property forfeit, but though the policy of suppression was pursued with vigour they were still undefeated in 410 when an imperial 'mediator' was despatched to Africa in the person of the count Marcellinus. Under his authority a conference was called to Carthage where eventually 286 Catholic and 284 Donatist bishops met on June 1st, 411. The result was a renewed ban on Donatism whose assemblies were forbidden, property confiscated and clergy exiled. As a consequence many came over to the opposing allegiance, but throughout the seventeen years which remained of Roman rule in Africa, 412–29, the struggle continued, nor was there any sign of its end when Augustine died in 430. Indeed there are traces of Donatism still active in the seventh century, and its final disappearance coincided with the destruction of Catholicism when both were swept away by Islam, each greatly weakened by the fruitless struggle in which they had been for so long engaged. The dire effects of schism are nowhere more clearly revealed, and the almost nonexistence of Christianity in North Africa today owes not a little to this division which sprang from the Persecutions, although economic and national factors helped so much to perpetuate it.

In Egypt where these factors were less operative and where Catholic Christianity had a greater hold on the native population a similar schism had a much shorter history. Here in 305 Melitius, bishop of Lycopolis in Upper Egypt, took upon himself both to ordain clergy in dioceses other than his own and to seek the support of the presbyters of Alexandria during the absence of its bishop, Peter, who was in hiding as a consequence of the Diocletian persecution. It is possible that Melitius was prompted by a desire to ensure the continued life of the Church in the emergency, but more probable that he acted from personal ambition to achieve pre-eminence over the metropolitan authority of Alexandria. To this motive he added further, like Novatian before him and the contemporary

Donatists, the rigorist plea when in 306 Peter issued an encyclical specifying graded penances for the lapsed. He was declared deposed by a synod meeting in Alexandria, but his condemnation to the mines, first in Egypt and then in Palestine, brought him the renown of a confessor, and upon his release, under the toleration edict of Galerius in 311, he consecrated a number of bishops, so that by 325 his 'church' had twenty-eight of them.

The Melitians seriously compromised their position when they joined the Arians against Athanasius and to discredit him brought forward certain charges in 331. They asserted that Athanasius had sent one of his presbyters to stop the services conducted by a certain Ischyras, that this envoy had found him in church celebrating the Eucharist, had thrown down the altar, smashed the chalice and burnt the church-books, thus perpetrating an act of sacrilege. Athanasius was able to prove that Ischyras was not in orders, that on the occasion in question he was ill in bed and that there was not a single chalice in the village. Equally unfounded was the further accusation that Athanasius had murdered a Melitian bishop, Arsenius, and had cut off his hand for magical purposes—the hand being produced as an exhibit. Athanasius, his information gained from a conversation overheard by servants in a tavern, was able both to find and produce Arsenius, alive and unmaimed. Such conduct and their Arian alliance alienated most Egyptians from the Melitians, especially as the monks, who were beginning to abound and were the objects of general admiration, were in the main orthodox and staunch supporters of the Nicene party. Nevertheless Melitianism managed to survive into the fifth century, although it at no time constituted a serious threat to Church unity.

The same cannot be said of the Meletian schism at Antioch, which stemmed not from persecution from without but from heresy within; in this case Arianism, i.e. the belief that Jesus was not fully God but only the most perfect of God's creatures. In 328 Eustathius, bishop of Antioch, a strong supporter of the Council of Nicaea at which Arianism had been condemned, was deposed and banished by means of a court intrigue. His immediate successors, Euphronius and Flacillus (332–42), were not openly heretical but they were suspected to be such, and a small group, under the presbyter Paulinus, refused to recognize them. About 360 Meletius was consecrated to the see, and in his first sermon was beginning to express his acceptance of the orthodox position when his archdeacon clapped a hand over his mouth to prevent further utterance. Meletius, not to be deterred, continued his affirmation in dumb show by extending first three fingers and then one to intimate his belief in the Trinity in unity. The semi-Arians, enraged by this, managed to procure his exile and had him replaced by Euzoius. The majority of the orthodox remained faithful to Meletius, but Paulinus' group, aware that Meletius had originally been a semi-Arian and indeed had owed his election to that fact, were not satisfied, despite his recent conduct, of his doctrinal purity and remained isolated.

Upon Julian's accession Meletius was allowed to return, and so in 362 a council met in Alexandria, presided over by Athanasius, which directed Paulinus and his flock to offer their communion to Meletius as long as he would anathematize Arius and profess the Nicene faith. Meanwhile Lucifer of Cagliari, exiled from his western Sardinian diocese for his pro-Nicene sympathies, a veritable firebrand and entirely uncompromising, arrived at Antioch and proceeded to consecrate Paulinus as bishop. Athanasius had perforce to choose between Paulinus and Meletius and hearing that the latter had entered into relations with the semi-Arians again recognized Paulinus. There were thus three bishops of Antioch: Euzoius accepted by the heretics, Paulinus accepted by Egypt and the West, and Meletius accepted by the remainder of the orthodox East.

It was in vain that Basil of Caesarea wrote to Athanasius to seek peace and sent deputations to the West. Damasus, bishop of Rome, and his advisers were ill-informed on Eastern affairs, and did not appreciate the need for unity against the Arians without too much insistence upon past errors which had been renounced. So, in a somewhat high-handed manner, a letter was sent to Paulinus, in 375, declaring that he alone was in communion with the West.

Three years later Euzoius died and no successor was appointed, so that by 381 it seemed to the local clergy that the opportunity was favourable to bring the schism to an end, and they undertook to advance no claim to the bishopric on the death of either Meletius or Paulinus but to accept the survivor. Unfortunately when Meletius died, shortly after this agreement had been reached, while attending the Council of Constantinople, the other delegates refused to acknowledge Paulinus on the grounds that this would mean a capitulation to the West which persisted in recognizing him, and they elected Flavian. In 388 Paulinus died, but as he had previously consecrated one Evagrius to succeed him, the schism continued: Egypt and the West accepting him and the East in general accepting Flavian.

In 391 both Flavian and Evagrius were summoned to the Synod of Capua; the former however excused himself on account of his age and the latter, though present, was unable to press his case, it being referred to the jurisdiction of Theophilus of Alexandria. Flavian, who saw in this a move that might be prejudicial to himself, sought to have the matter settled through his influence at court and succeeded in securing his position. Evagrius was condemned, only to die shortly afterwards. Flavian was then accepted by Theophilus and through him communion was re-established between Antioch and Rome. The strict Catholic group continued, bishopless, until it was finally reconciled in 414.

This outline history of some of the leading and most representative schisms, which is by no means exhaustive—there were also for example the Luciferian schism, centring mainly in Spain, the Felician in Gaul as well as the various papal schisms from Hippolytus and Callistus (217) to Eulalius and Zosimus (418)—reveals the divided nature of Christendom even in the early centuries. The disciplinary problems arising from these divisions had a profound effect upon the doctrine of the sacraments and the ministry, and were no doubt a contributing factor to the growth of papal supremacy in the West as a focus of unity. They affected too the doctrine of the Church which with a rigid exclusivism, at times justified, maintained the conviction of its undivided nature by declaring that all schism was outside itself. The schisms too were an ominous presage of the later Great Schism when in the eleventh, twelfth and thirteenth centuries East and West finally split, and even of the as yet far distant Reformation when the West itself was further subdivided. This is an element which should perhaps be listed under the unmaking rather than the making of the Church, for such action clearly went against the intention of its Founder and seemed to make nonsense of the claim that in Christ all are one.

5

The Social Life of the Church

ONE of the most characteristic features of the first-century Palestinian Judaism in which Christianity was nurtured was the barrier erected between the members of the chosen people and the Gentiles. If some, in particular the Jews of the Dispersion, occasionally sat light to this distinction, the prevailing Hebrew attitude was one of rigorous exclusivism. It is true that the Temple at Jerusalem had its Court of the Gentiles, but the mere suggestion that the more sacred precincts had been violated by Paul's introduction of the Ephesian Trophimus was sufficient to cause a riot. Indeed the Gentile could only truly approach God by ceasing to be a Gentile; he had, that is to say, to become in effect a naturalized Jew by rites of purification and circumcision. This division related not only to the more specifically religious acts but to all aspects of social life. Contact with the Gentiles was as far as was humanly possible to be avoided.

This social dualism was perpetuated in the early Church, albeit on a different basis once the struggle to allow the Gentiles entrance had been won. The division was now no longer a racial one, but essentially religious, between the worshippers of the one true God and those who accepted polytheism. The Christian, as we have noted previously, was in the world but not of it, a sojourner and a pilgrim; to Tertullian he was 'a foreigner in this world, a citizen of Jerusalem, the city above'.

Thus as Israel of old, so the Church remained a people apart, obedient to the government, but hostile to imperial culture and having no real share in the life of secular society invested as it was at every turn with the sanctions and appurtenances of the pagan cults.

It was not that the Christian wished to have nothing to do with his neighbour because he felt himself superior to him, but that his neighbour lived in an aura of idolatry which spread to every aspect of his social life. Since the Christian was expected to give up all that savoured of idolatry, he was inevitably circumscribed and cut off from contact with many of his fellow citizens. How could the Christian be a magistrate when that office involved libations and sacrifices? How could he join the army when that necessitated his presence at pagan rites? How could he even sign a contract with a non-believer when the normal form included the names of certain gods? How could he attend the games which honoured the Olympian deities? How could he accept an invitation to dinner when those he considered to be but demons would be the subjects of toasts? If he could not avoid occasional mention of the gods, as for instance when asked the way he must reply 'He lives near the temple of Aesculapius' or 'I live in Isis street', he could at least absent himself from gatherings where every oath was an appeal to the gods of the nations.

In the Apostolic Age Christians had been disturbed as to whether or not they should eat meat bought in the public market, whose main supply consisted of the victims offered in the temples, and though, with Paul, the majority came to see that such matters were indifferent, they did consider that they could not engage either in work or recreation which might serve not only to condone but even to encourage false religion. Consequently from the earliest days there were certain professions which a Christian might not adopt or might not continue to practise once he had become a member of the Church.

A comprehensive list of these, which gathers together the substance of earlier injunctions, is to be found in the *Apostolic Constitutions*:

If any one be a maintainer of harlots, let him either leave off to prostitute women, or else let him be rejected. If a harlot come, let her leave off whoredom, or else let her be rejected. If a maker of idols come, let him either leave off his employment, or let him be rejected. If one belonging to a theatre come, whether it be man or woman, or a charioteer or dueller or racer or Olympic gamester, or one that plays on the pipe or the lute or on the harp at those games, or a dancing-master or an huckster, either let them leave off their employments, or let them be rejected. If a soldier come, let him be taught 'to do no injustice, to accuse no man falsely, and to be content with his allotted wages': if he submit to these rules, let him be received; but if he refuse them, let him be rejected. He that is guilty of sins not to be named, a sodomite, an astrologer, a diviner, a user of magic verses, a juggler, a mountebank, one that makes amulets, a charmer, a soothsayer, a fortune-teller, an observer of palmistry; he, that when he meets you, observes defects in the eyes or feet of birds or cats, or noises or symbolical sounds; let these be proved for some time, for this sort of wickedness is hard to be washed away; and if they leave off those practices, let them be received; but if they will not agree to that, let them be rejected. . . . Let him that follows the Gentile customs, or Jewish fables, either reform, or let him be rejected. If any one follows the sport of the theatre, their huntings, or horse-races, or combats, either let him leave them off, or let him be rejected.

But even this list does not exhaust all the possibilities of contact with idolatry. So Tertullian was concerned to point out that plasterers, painters, marble-workers, workers in bronze, engravers and carpenters might all be expected to process images or adorn temples or produce artefacts bearing the likeness and insignia of the gods. The professor of literature and schoolmaster too could not but teach the legends of which classical literature is so full. The seller of incense might be providing fuel for altars. 'No art, no profession, no trade,' affirms Tertullian, 'which adminsters either to equipping or forming idols, can be free from the title of idolatry.' This did not mean that there was nothing a Christian might legitimately undertake, but it did require a constant vigilance to see that none of the commodities and services in which he dealt were in any way an adjunct to the cults of polytheism.

It is not surprising therefore to learn that many converts found life hard and many too were willing to change their religious allegiance without altering their previous mode of life. Tertullian again informs us of the kind of excuses they advanced: 'I shall be in need.' 'I shall have no food.' 'My work was my subsistence.' 'Provision must be made for children and posterity.' 'I was under contract.' Some even tried to argue from Scripture: 'Paul said, "Let each man abide in that calling wherein he was called." '

But if some Christians found it difficult to pursue a trade, the majority were able to obtain an adequate means of livelihood, and they were to be found in all kinds of occupation. From the New Testament we hear of a tanner, a centurion, a seller of purple, a jailor, a lawyer, a doctor and household servants. Later funerary inscriptions refer to gardeners, barbers, sailors, millers, butchers, linen-makers, builders of organs, blacksmiths—indeed the list could be extended indefinitely. Yet initially Christianity was primarily a movement of the lower classes in which slaves, freedmen and labourers predominated. Hence Paul's statement that 'not many wise after the flesh, not many mighty, not many noble, are called'. Permeation of the upper classes was slow but steady: by the opening of the second century Pliny could report that 'many of all ranks' in Bithynia had gone over to the Christian sect, while by the reign of Commodus large numbers, according to Eusebius, 'even of those at Rome, highly distinguished for wealth and birth, were advancing towards their own salvation with all their households and kindred'.

If the actual methods of work adopted by Christians differed in no particulars from those of their pagan contemporaries, their attitude was essentially distinct. To the Greeks of the pre-Christian era work was a servile activity, fit only for the masses who thereby provided the citizens with the leisure they required for political pursuits and the acquisition of virtue. The Romans accepted this point of view and equally regarded work as beneath the dignity of a citizen. Hence the frequent jibes at the Church because most of its members were artisans. The Stoic ideal of the brotherhood of men helped a little to remove the stigma of slavery and so of the work connected with it, but it was the Church above all that gave to labour a sense of purpose and direction.

Mindful of the fact that their Master had been a carpenter and that many of the apostles had plied trades, the early Christians stressed the need for work and Paul enunciated the principle: 'If any will not work, neither let him eat.' For the Christian therefore there was to be no idling and the motives of his efforts were, first, that he might not be a burden on others; second, that he might thereby provide for others less fortunate than himself; third, that he might achieve peace and tranquillity of spirit in the execution of his tasks, and, finally, that he might thereby serve God. 'Whatsoever ye do, work heartily, as unto the Lord, and not unto men; knowing that from the Lord ye shall receive the recompense of the inheritance; ye serve the Lord Christ.'

So important was the duty of work that in the *Didache*, a second century manual of practical instructions concerning Church life, it was asserted that should a visiting Christian not be prepared to earn his keep his faith was suspect, and conversely that the local church was to provide the opportunity for work when such people came to their community.

The increase in the number of cultured and rich folk entering the Church, accelerated by the conversion of Constantine,
tended to bring back into prominence the ancient pagan contempt for labour. But the leaders of the Church would have
none of it; hence the strictures of John Chrysostom:

When you see a man driving nails, smiting with a hammer,
covered with soot, do not consider him cheap, but rather for that
reason admire him. For even Peter girded himself, and handled the
dragnet, and went fishing after the Lord's Resurrection. And why
say I Peter? Paul himself, standing in a tent-maker's shop, sewed
hides together, while angels were reverencing him and demons
quaking with fear. Nor was he ashamed to say, 'These hands
ministered unto my necessities, and to them that were with me.'
Did I say that he was not ashamed? Rather, he gloried in this very
fact.

Yet if the Church inculcated in its members a high esteem
for work, it made no protest against the institution of slavery
under which, since the free labourer had virtually disappeared
due to economic pressure, most work was done. Nevertheless,
apart from some isolated exceptions, the attitude of Christians
to slaves differed radically from that of pagan masters. 'Implements,' according to the Roman Varro, 'are of three kinds:
vocal, including slaves; semi-vocal, e.g. oxen, and dumb, for
instance ploughs.' By contrast the Christian Clement of Alexandria († c. 215) could say, 'Slaves are men like ourselves,' and
Lactantius declared that 'slaves are not slaves to us. We deem
them brothers after the spirit, in religion fellow-servants.'
This follows logically from the Pauline thesis that 'there can
be neither Jew nor Greek, there can be neither bond nor free,
there can be no male and female: for ye all are one in Christ
Jesus.' Thus before God all those in Christ are equal and the
Church's task is to preach humanity to the employers and
good behaviour to the slaves. So little prejudice existed

concerning this that a slave could attain the highest office in the Church, e.g. Callistus who became bishop of Rome in 217. Indeed the disregard of any distinction between slave and free man is illustrated by the complete absence of the term from the many Christian epitaphs of the period.

The influx of new members in the fourth century was not without its effects in this as in so many other particulars. Many of the rich were slow to cast off the ideas of their earlier pagan life, hence the Church had constantly to reaffirm the principle of religious equality. 'Think not, you rich,' declared Gregory of Nazianzus, 'that it is beneath your dignity to be baptized with the poor, or you masters with your slaves. For even in so doing you humble not yourselves as did Christ, in whom you are this day baptized, and who, for your sakes, took upon him the form of a slave. For, from the day that you are changed anew, all the ancient marks disappear; Christ is impressed as a common form on all.' In similar vein Chrysostom affirmed the equality of the partakers of the sacrament of the Lord's Supper. The Church's efforts were thus mainly centred in the amelioration of the conditions of the slaves and the teaching that they were as much members of the Church, with the certain hope of immortality, as any one else in the social scale.

Life then was, no more than in the twentieth century, not all work and no play, but even in the matter of recreations the Christian was to be distinguished from the pagan. The public amusements of the populace consisted of the theatre, gladiatorial combats, horse-racing and circuses.

The era of the great classical plays was largely over and in their place the theatres presented gross comedies, indecent ballets and ribald pantomimes. Hence Tertullian could refer to them, in typically epigrammatic fashion, as 'immodesty's own peculiar abode', while Chrysostom could assert that to allow children to attend was to subject them to the danger of suffering utter corruption through eyes and ears. Here indeed one was given lessons in adultery, the tragedies being bloody and the comedies wanton. From time to time too farces were put on which parodied Christian beliefs. In one, the principal character lay on his back as if ill and called loudly for baptism, complaining that he felt heavy and wanted to be made light. 'How is that to be done?' asked the other performers. 'Do you think we are carpenters and are going to plane you down?' 'Fools,' cried the chief player, 'I want to die a Christian.' His desire was nearer fulfilment than he expected, for no sooner had a mock priest and an exorcist appeared on the scene and baptized him, than soldiers entered and carried him off to the judge to answer for his new religion, and he was condemned to death. The Fathers of the Church were therefore constantly attacking these spectacles arguing that as Jesus had said, 'Every one that looketh on a woman to lust after her hath committed adultery with her already in his heart,' the presence of a believer at such displays must inevitably issue in sin. Yet human nature being loath to restrict its pleasures, there were not a few backsliders in the early centuries and their number increased with the passage of time, so that by the middle of the fifth century we find Salvian complaining bitterly:

There is no doubt that we love that the more which we put first. For on every day of these deadly sports, if there happens to be any feasts of the Church, they who call themselves Christians do not only not come to church; but if, by chance, not having heard of any such thing, they have come, as soon as ever they hear there are plays, they presently leave the church. The church of God is despised that they may haste to the play-house: the church emptied, the circus filled. We leave Christ on the altar that we may feed our eyes, that run awhoring after the unclean sights, with the fornication of those filthy pastimes.

The Christian ideal was nevertheless complete abstention and this applied equally to the shows in the amphitheatre.

There were combats between a *retiarius*, armed with net and trident, and a *murmillo* carrying a short sword, and between a Thracian with dagger and round shield and a Samnite with sword and oblong shield. Victims, often Christians, were thrown to wild beasts to be torn to pieces while the crowd howled its blood-lust. 'Cannibal banquets for the soul' is how Tertullian described them in condemning them. But it was horse-racing that called forth the greatest popular hysteria. Heated debates concerning pedigrees and the chances of the different runners, clashes between the factions sporting the colours of rival charioteers, gambling fever of the utmost intensity—all these ran counter to that tranquillity of spirit which a Christian sought to evince. The rivalry, rage, bitterness, grief and spiritual agitation which were the invariable accompaniments of races were far from the peace which was numbered among the fruit of the Spirit. There was further the idolatry inseparable from these meetings—sacrifices preceded them; the chariot and pair were consecrated to the moon, the chariot and four to the sun; the eggs which marked the beginning of the laps were sacred to Ceres and the dolphins which showed their completion were in honour of Neptune. No wonder that Clement of Alexandria should declare:

If people shall say that they betake themselves to the spectacles as a pastime for recreation, I should say that the cities which make a serious business of pastime are not wise; for cruel contests for glory which have been so fatal are not sport. No more is senseless expenditure of money, nor are the riots that are occasioned by them sport. And ease of mind is not to be purchased by zealous pursuit of frivolities, for no one who has his senses will ever prefer what is pleasant to what is good.

The more private pursuits of the populace quite naturally had the same character as their public amusements. Much time was spent in gossip in the baths, in barbers' shops and in taverns. Gambling at home was a frequent pastime and the throwing of dice was much favoured. The highest throw, the 'Venus', was when all the dice showed different points; the lowest when all turned up aces. Other casts had similar names, adopted from gods or heroes, such as 'Stesichorus' which was the two aces and the two trays. Gambling-tables of ivory, carefully engraved with inscriptions, were a usual household requisite. But the Church would have none of this, convinced that the test of a man's spiritual health was the tone and temper of his leisure hours. So the Council of Elvira ordered a year's penance for those who joined in games of chance and Clement of Alexandria, to quote him once more, was quite emphatic:

Let not men therefore spend their time in barbers' shops and taverns, babbling nonsense; and let them give up hunting for the women who pass by, and ceaselessly talking slander against many to raise a laugh. The game of dice is to be prohibited, and the pursuit of gain, especially by dicing, which many keenly follow. Such things the prodigality of luxury invents for the idle. For the cause is idleness, and a love for frivolities apart from the truth. For it is not possible otherwise to obtain enjoyment without injury; and each man's preference of a mode of life is a counterpart of his disposition.

What then did the Christian do in his leisure time? To a certain extent he occupied himself with what would be called today good works, that is to say he visited the sick, sought to relieve the necessities of the poor and generally revealed his love for the brethren by spending his time in their company. He was encouraged to go for country walks, to engage in a little fishing, to undertake bodily exercise, even gymnastics; not, says Clement, 'that we are to struggle with cunning and showiness, but in a stand-up wrestling bout, by disentangling of neck, hands and sides. For such a struggle with graceful strength is more becoming and manly, being undertaken for the sake of serviceable and profitable health.' The women were not expected to indulge in such physical effort but to spin or weave or superintend the cooking. Parents were to look after their children, telling them stories, teaching them to read and write and to pray. Reading aloud was constantly recommended, and the Christian had a choice between the Scriptures, which were expected to be his primary study, and the many apocryphal works containing stories of the apostles which were the novels of the early Church. Books themselves were not particularly dear to buy, for not only was there neither copyright nor royalties to pay, but it was easy for one person to dictate to any number of scribes at once and the publisher did not have to find wages for his own slaves. Nearly every church too had its library—even the small house-church of Cirta in North Africa had one at the beginning of the fourth century—and there was much lending and borrowing among the members of a congregation. In time however the Church adopted a very strict attitude to reading. 'Anything that is not read in the churches should not be read privately,' Cyril of Jerusalem told his candidates for baptism c. 350. 'Deceive not your soul with strange books,' was the advice of Gregory of Nazianzus. Despite the protests of Priscillian in Spain at the end of the century the apocryphal works gradually disappeared from the shelves and reading became more and more confined, although this was in part offset by the publication of lives of the saints and in particular of the great ascetics. So the *Life of Antony* by Athanasius, written between 356 and 362, became a bestseller, being immediately translated into Latin and also going through Syriac, Armenian and Arabic editions. Again the *Life of Martin* by Sulpicius Severus, c. 395, was known throughout the length and breadth of the Mediterranean world.

So the Christian man and woman lived together in the bosom of their family, in close contact with the local community of which they were members, and sought to shield themselves from the temptations and disturbances of the secular world. Moderation and simplicity were their watchwords and this is nowhere better exemplified than in their attitude to food and clothing. The pagans of the early centuries were notorious for their gluttony and general lack of temperance. In the *Satyricon* of Petronius, *c.* A.D. 60, a very detailed account is given of a dinner party at the house of one Trimalchio. Since this provides a most vivid picture of pagan indulgence, a paraphrased summary of what took place will serve as a useful background to the Christian viewpoint.

The guests had hardly taken their place in the dining-room when some Alexandrian slaves came and poured iced water over their hands, while a chiropodist pared their toe-nails. They sang the whole time; in fact the attendants sang so that it might be thought to be a theatre rather than a room in a gentleman's private house. The hors d'œuvres were served magnificently: on a tray was an ass, made of Corinthian bronze, with two panniers containing black and white olives; on either side of that were two dishes, engraved with Trimalchio's name and the weight of the silver. Then there were dormice sprinkled with honey and poppy-seeds, sausages smoking hot on a silver gridiron and damsons and sliced pomegranates.

Then a flourish of music was heard and the host was carried in. He was followed by a basket with a sitting hen of wood in it. Two slaves rummaged in the straw and provided all present with a peafowl's egg, made out of pastry: inside the yolk was hidden a fine, plump beccafico, seasoned with pepper. The next item was a silver skeleton, so constructed that its joints and backbone could be twisted in any way one liked. Trimalchio proceeded to make a solemn speech on the mortality of man, and, during the ensuing applause, a round tray was carried in encircled with the signs of the Zodiac, and on each sign was an appropriate delicacy. So over the Bull was a piece of beef, over the Twins a pair of sweetbreads and kidneys, and on the Scales a balance with a tart in one pan and a

cheesecake in the other. Off came the top of this tray and under-
neath was a hare with wings attached to look like Pegasus, while at
each corner were four figures of Marsyas with sauce dripping from
their bellies into a canal in which fish were floating.

A boar was carried in next, at which the host looked carefully
and then declared it had not been properly gutted. The cook was
dragged in and stripped on the spot, while two torturers stood by.
The guests interceded for him, and Trimalchio agreed to pardon
him if he cleaned the pig there and then. The chef sliced open the
paunch and out came tumbling sausages and black-puddings. There
was something unexpected at every turn. Rope dancers and jugglers
paraded in: lottery tickets were handed out and all received
individual gifts. But the grand spectacle of the evening was still to
come. Suddenly the panelled ceiling began to creak and the whole
house shook. Then the panelling divided and a huge ring descended,
with gold chaplets and jars of perfume hanging all round the edge.
They were more presents to take home.

It must of course be acknowledged that this is a satire upon
the behaviour of a *nouveau riche*, but though in particulars it
is exaggerated there is sufficient substratum of truth to make it
a not unfair description of contemporary pagan subjection to
what Christians called the 'Belly-Demon'. It is indeed true
that the world was swept as if with a drag-net to gratify the
jaded palates of the well-to-do. Lampreys from the Straits of
Sicily; oysters from Abydos; sprats from Lipara; turnips from
Mantinea; cockles from Methymna; turbots from Attica; peafowl of Media; mullets from Sciathus; thrushes from Daphnis;
chicken from Phasis; almonds of Perekh—all these weighed
down the patrician tables. As for wines—or 'Bacchic fuel' as
the Christian termed it—different types hailed from Lesbos,
Crete, Syracuse and Italy. All these, as we have seen from
Petronius' account, were served with a magnificence which
spared no expense—silver and gold plate was common; there
were knives with forged Indian steel blades and ivory handles;

the guests reclined on ivory-footed couches, with fine linen tablecloths, silver sideboards and splendid draperies. It is little wonder that the Christians went to an almost Puritanical extreme in their condemnation of these extravagances and in their practice of a much simpler manner of life.

The Church's attitude can be succinctly expressed. The Christian does not live to eat but eats to live and preserve his health and strength. 'Neither is food our business, nor pleasure our aim,' states Clement, 'but both are on account of our life here, which the Son of God is training up to immortality.' The Christian too must be free from all subservience to material things. 'The smells of the kitchen may induce us to eat,' acknowledges Jerome († 420), 'but when hunger is satisfied they make us their slaves. Hence gorging gives rise to disease: and many persons find relief for the discomfort of gluttony in emetics—what they disgraced themselves by putting in, they with still greater disgrace put out.' So the Christian diet consisted of dishes requiring no elaborate preparation—beans, olives, fish, cheese, apples, bread, milk or water. A little wine was admissible in cold weather or as a medicine, but children should not be allowed to touch it. Both food and drink were to be served in earthenware vessels, and the implements should be plain and not ornate. This frugality was considered to be all the more necessary because the money thereby saved, of which the Christian was regarded as not the owner but the steward, could be devoted to charitable ends.

All this does not mean that Christians did not have dinner parties; not only were they encouraged to be generous in hospitality, but they met together regularly for what may be termed Church supper-parties. These agapes, as they were called, would seem to have derived from the Last Supper. The communion service, as we shall see in a succeeding chapter, was at first a repetition of the whole of the Last Supper, meal included. In time however, partly due to certain excesses which accompanied the meal, the bread and the cup were dissociated and the meal was continued on its own as a fellowship gathering. For a full description we may turn to the account given by Hippolytus:

And the bishop, having broken the bread, must on all occasions taste of it, and eat with such of the faithful as are present. And they shall take from the hand of the bishop one fragment of a loaf before each takes his own bread, for this is the 'blessed bread'. But it is not the Eucharist, as is the Body of the Lord.

And before they drink let each of those present take a cup and give thanks and drink; and so let the baptized take their meal.

But to the catechumens let exorcized bread be given, and they each for themselves offer a cup. A catechumen shall not sit at table at the Lord's Supper.

And throughout the meal let him who eats remember him who invited him, for he was invited to the latter's home for that very purpose. But when you eat and drink, do so in an orderly manner and not so that any one may mock, or your host be saddened by your unruliness, but behave so that he may pray to be worthy that the saints may enter his dwelling: 'For ye,' it is said, 'are the salt of the earth.'

If you are all assembled and offered something to be taken away, accept it from your host and depart. But if all are to eat then and there, do not eat to excess, so that your host may send some of what the saints leave to whomsoever he will, and he to whom it is sent may rejoice in what is left over.

But while the guests are eating, let them eat silently, not arguing but attending to such things as the bishop may teach, and if any one asks him a question let an answer be given him.

And even if the bishop should be absent when the faithful meet at a supper, if a presbyter or a deacon is present they shall eat in a similarly orderly fashion, and each shall be careful to take the blessed bread from the presbyter's or deacon's hand; and in the same way the catechumens shall take the exorcized bread.

But if only laymen meet, let them not act presumptuously, for a layman cannot bless the blessed bread.

Let each one eat in the name of the Lord; for this is pleasing to the Lord that we should be jealous of our good name even among the heathen, all sober alike.

If at any times anyone wishes to invite the widows, let him feed them and send them away before sunset. But if, on account of existing conditions, he cannot entertain them at his house, let him send them away, and they may eat of his food at their homes in any way they please.

Common to all agapes was the breaking and blessing of bread at the beginning, but otherwise there was considerable diversity in different places, the reason of which is not difficult to discover. Once the meal ceased to be joined to the Eucharist, it assumed the character of a private party and although the bishop or some other member of the clergy was usually invited and expected to preside, it ceased to be under the direct control of the Church authorities. This would be especially the case as the number of occasions when the agape was celebrated increased. But since the arrangements lay in private hands, each one would be free, within certain limits, to follow what order he chose and hence the difference in practice.

Love-feasts were held on three main occasions. At marriages, *agapes connubiales*, at funerals, *agapes funerales*, and on the feast days of martyrs, *agapes natalitiae*. But with the rapid increase in Church membership, the primitive sense of brotherhood became less acute and social distinctions began to reassert themselves, so that the agape developed into a social entertainment for the wealthy or a mere dole of food for the poor. As early as the beginning of the third century, Tertullian, turned Montanist, condemned the lasciviousness and intemperance which had crept into the observance; nor were the clergy free from blame, since they readily accepted a double portion of meat and drink. Clement of Alexandria protested against the immodest revelry and his objection to the use of flutes indicates that instrumental music of a secular character had replaced the psalms and spiritual songs of earlier days. Gregory of Nazianzus was led to complain: 'If we come together to satisfy the belly and to enjoy the changing and fleeting pleasures, and so turn this place of temperance into a place of gluttony and satiety . . . I do not see how our conduct corresponds with the occasion.' Augustine saw the bad effects which such behaviour would have on the proclamation of the Gospel because 'those debaucheries and lavish banquets in cemeteries are usually believed by a sensual and ignorant populace to be not only commemorations of martyrs, but even consolations to the dead'. 'These drunkards,' he declared, 'persecute the saints as much with cups as the furious pagans did with stones.'

The official attitude of the Church, as distinct from that of individuals, was formulated in numerous canons at successive councils. The Synod of Gangra, c. 353, found it necessary, in order to foster the holding of the agape, to condemn those who refused to take part out of disgust at the behaviour sometimes witnessed. But ten years later, influenced by the growing reverence for church-buildings as places of worship, the Council of Laodicea forbade their use for agapes. In 397 the third Council of Carthage not only repeated this injunction but also ordered that all Christians should 'as far as possible be debarred from entertainments of this kind'. The bishops took steps to implement these canons; Ambrose at Milan instructed the doorkeepers to turn away anyone bringing food and Augustine wrote to Valerius, bishop of Hippo, to induce him to follow Ambrose's example, for the agape had become indistinguishable from heathen banquets and was therefore to be discouraged. Nevertheless the agape still persisted and in the same year as the Council of Carthage, Pammachius held a great funeral banquet in the basilica of St. Peter's at Rome in honour of his deceased mother Paulina. In the fifth century common meals were held in the Thebaid every Saturday night and Theodoret reports yearly feasting in honour of the martyrs. Gregory the Great was prepared to allow them at the dedication of churches, particularly in the case of the newly converted English. Even after the final condemnation, under Justinian II, at the Trullan or 'Quinisextan' Council of 692, traces of it still persisted in the *eulogia* or blessed bread taken to absent members of the congregation.

Here in miniature is the record of a process of secularization, from the solemn and decorous meals of the early Church, so sharply in contrast to pagan convivial gatherings, to the unlicensed festivities of the later fourth century which were indistinguishable from those of the pagans. A similar process is to be seen in the matter of clothing and personal adornment.

Within the New Testament itself we find the expression of Christian distaste at vulgar display and excessive concern for personal appearance. Women are exhorted, in I Timothy, to adorn themselves 'in modest apparel, with shamefastness and sobriety; not with braided hair, and gold or pearls or costly raiment'. While in I Peter wives are told to deck themselves not with 'the outward adorning of plaiting the hair, and of wearing jewels of gold, or of putting on apparel; but let it be the hidden man of the heart, in the incorruptible apparel of a meek and quiet spirit, which is in the sight of God of great price'.

The principles upon which the Church based its opposition to the extravagances of contemporary fashion were sixfold. First, it offended humility since it was obviously ostentatious and self-regarding; second, it undermined chastity, since it stimulated lustful thoughts in the mind of the beholder; third, it was a sign of intemperance and lack of self-control; fourth, it required so much effort and time which would be better spent in spiritual exercises; fifth, it was costly, women carrying in their ears and on their necks objects of great value, and this money should be used for succouring the needy; sixth, it ran counter to the Christian indifference to the world, and finally, in close association with this, it weakened self-discipline and so rendered the believer less capable of facing the trials which, when persecution was always a possibility, he or she might at any time be required to face.

For such delicacies [says Tertullian], as tend by their softness and effeminacy to unman the manliness of faith are to be discarded. Otherwise, I know not whether the wrist that is used to being surrounded with the palm-leaf-like bracelet will endure till it grow into the numb hardness of its own chain. I know not whether the leg that has rejoiced in the anklet will suffer itself to be squeezed into the gyve. I fear the neck, beset with pearls and emerald nooses, will give no room to the broadsword. Wherefore, let us meditate on hardships, and we shall not feel them: let us abandon luxuries, and we shall not regret them.

The Fathers of the Church in the ante-Nicene period conducted an incessant campaign against pagan fashion, pouring scorn, for example, upon the fantastic hair styles which kept women awake all night for fear that in their sleep they should disarrange what it had taken the most of the day to put in order. Cosmetics, whereby the prostitute was imitated, were equally condemned. Simplicity was the hallmark of the Christian. Instead of the brilliantly coloured Indian silk dresses and the gold-plated sandals, the Christian woman was expected to put on a white woollen tunic and untrimmed shoes. Instead of tresses, wigs and dyeings, she bound her hair simply along the neck with a plain pin. Considering that the best decoration for the ear was true instruction, she refrained from the lobe-piercing which permitted the use of rings and drops; and confident that a woman should be adorned within and not without, she disdained chains, collars, rings and bracelets. The temptation to such outward show was rendered less by her absence from the many public shows and gatherings, with their invariable idolatrous accompaniments, but within her home it was permissible to relax some of the strictness of dress and behaviour that should normally characterize her. So she might adorn herself a little to please her husband, as long as her intention was to secure his admiration and not devote herself to mere personal ostentation. She might too, for the same purpose, employ a few perfumes, though not too many nor those that were overpowering. Again she might wear a modicum of jewellery, such as a signet ring, which was after all useful for sealing things to be kept safe at home. But in this, as in all other matters, excess was to be avoided.

The Christian man too was required to abstain from the effeminate toilet affected by so many. He had not, according to Tertullian, 'to cut the beard too sharply; to pluck it out here and there; to shave round about the mouth; to arrange the hair, and disguise its hoariness by dyes; to remove all the incipient down all over the body; to fix each hair in its place with womanly pigment; to smooth all the rest of the body by the aid of some rough powder or other'. His clothes were to be clean, simple and neat. Normally he wore a *tunica alba*, a white garment reaching nearly to the ground with long sleeves; a *paenula*, a semicircular piece of material fastened down the centre front with an opening for the head, and around his neck an *orarium* or small towel with which to wipe his hands or his mouth. It was indeed these same three articles of dress that in the course of time, through stylization, developed into the vestments of the celebrant at the Eucharist—the *tunica* becoming the alb, the *paenula* the chasuble and the *orarium* the stole.

If too great a concern for admiration and sartorial splendour was kept at bay during the early centuries, the later fourth century saw a greater readiness to compromise with worldly standards, which affected not only the general run of the faithful but even the widows and virgins despite their undertaking of a specific vocation. So Augustine could complain of some virgins: 'there is a certain air of pleasing, either by more elegant dress than the necessity of so great a profession demands, or by remarkable manners of binding the head, whether by bosses of hair swelling forth, or by coverings so unyielding that the fine net work below appears'. In similar vein Chrysostom said to them:

You may study appearances in a common garment more than those who wear gold. For when a very dark-coloured robe is drawn closely round the breast with the girdle, with such nicety that it may neither spread into the breadth nor shrink into scantiness, but be between both; and when the bosom is set off with many folds, is not this more alluring than any silken robes? And when the shoe, shining through its blackness, ends in a sharp point, and imitates the elegance of painting, so that even the breadth of the sole is hardly visible—or when, though you do not indeed paint your face, you spend much time and pains on washing it, and spread a veil across the forehead, whiter than the face itself—and above that put on a hood, of which the blackness may set off the white by contrast—is there not in all this the vanity of dress? What can one say to the perpetual rolling of the eyes? To the putting on of the stomacher so artfully as sometimes to disclose the fastening? For this too they sometimes expose, so as to shew the exquisiteness of the cincture, winding the hood entirely round the head. Then, like the players, they wear gloves so closely fitted that they seem to grow upon the hands.

And again:

There are indeed widows now; there are also virgins; but they do not retain that adornment which women should have who prepare themselves for such wrestling. For both the special distinction of the virgin is the caring for the things of God alone, and the waiting on him without distraction; and the widow's mark too should not be so much the not engaging in a second marriage, as the other things, charity to the poor, hospitality, continuing instant in prayer. One may see also the married women among us exhibiting great seemliness, but this is not the only thing required, but rather that sedulous attention to the needy through which those women of old shone out most brightly. Not as the generality nowadays. For then instead of gold they were clothed with the fair array of almsgiving; but now, having left off this, they are decked out on every side with cords of gold woven of the chain of their sins.

We see here evidence of the world pressing into the Church, its standards and modes of thought clashing with the Christian ideal of thought and conduct. This may be seen again in the superstitious practices which converts found so difficult to discard. Pagan society itself was shot through and through with such ideas. Many an after-dinner conversation was no more than the swapping of tales concerning hobgoblins, werewolves and witches. So of a man who had suddenly become rich, it was said that he had stolen a wishing cap from a hobgoblin and so was led to some treasure. The story was told of a man returning home with a friend who suddenly removed his clothes, at the roadside, and disappeared; upon reaching his house, the survivor was informed by his wife that a wolf had been savaging the sheep, only to be driven off with a spear thrust in the neck: going next to his friend's house, he heard the further news that he was in bed, with the doctor in attendance and an ugly wound in the neck. Again the tale went the rounds of the death of a slave and of the screeching of the night-witches as he lay awaiting burial: one brave man rushed out of the house only to return shortly covered with bruises and raving mad: the body of the dead boy, upon examination, was found to have vanished and in its place there remained a bundle of straw.

The convert could not easily rid himself of such beliefs, inculcated since childhood, and if he were confident in the power of Christ to protect him from evil spirits, he did not see that this prevented his making use of other precautions as well. So he would collect mud from the bottom of the baths and smear his children's foreheads to avert evil and jealousy; he would tie the names of rivers round them to ward off diseases; he would place a copy of the Gospels on their heads to cure a fever; he would attach names to several candles and use that for his child which was on the one that burned longest. Chrysostom lists further superstitions in order to condemn them:

How often one hears them saying: 'This or that man was the first to meet me as I walked out, consequently innumerable ills will certainly befall me; that confounded servant of mine, in giving me my shoes, handed me the left one first: this indicates dire calamities and insults; as I stepped out I started with the left foot foremost: this, too, is a sign of misfortune; my right eye twitched upwards as I went out: this portends tears. The braying of a donkey, the crowing of a cock, a sudden sneeze—all are omens of something. If one meets a virgin then one's journey will be barren, but if one meets a courtesan then it is certain to be fruitful.'

In close connexion with this over-credulous attitude notice should also be taken of the cult of relics. It was quite natural for Christians during the persecuting era to regard with veneration the mortal remains of those who had witnessed to the faith with their life-blood. So in the first extant acts of a martyr, those of Polycarp, it is recorded that the brethren 'took up his bones which are more valuable than precious stones and finer than refined gold and laid them in a suitable place'. Their intention was to hold an annual service at the tomb 'for the commemoration of those that have already fought in the contest and for the training and preparation of those that shall do so hereafter'. The expression of this quite normal human sentiment however was liable to distortion and when

peace came to the Church, with the unhindered opportunities
for celebrating the glorious past, the cult of the martyrs became
widely popular. Soon relics were regarded as providing a protection for the wearer—pieces of bone and splinters of the
Cross found their way into rings and amulets. The leaders of
the Church were not opposed to such practices and while they
were emphatic, with Jerome, that 'we honour the relics of the
martyrs that we may adore him whose martyrs they are', and
while they were very concerned to ensure authenticity and
condemned all purveyors of false relics, they did open the door
to a form of Christianized superstition which was to lead to
great abuse in the mediaeval period.

Yet if occasionally the Church authorities condoned a
limited number of largely pagan practices, they were inces-
santly active to combat the spirit of compromise. They were
well aware of the dangers to pure living and to the actualization
of the Christian ideal and they continued, as their predecessors,
to seek to apply the faith to every single aspect of life—nothing was to be outside the sphere of God's concern. Clement's
advice to the newly baptized, if indeed he be the author of this
brief fragment, may stand as a reminder of this ideal of
Christian living:

Practise quietness in word, quietness in deed, similarly in speech
and walking, and avoid impetuous haste. For then the mind will
remain steadfast, and will not be confused by your haste and so
become weak and devoid of practical wisdom and perceive
obscurely; nor will it be worsted by gluttony, worsted by boiling
rage, worsted by other passions, lying a ready prey for them. For
the mind, seated on high on a quiet throne, gazing intently at God,
must govern the passions. By no means be subject to sudden bursts
of temper in order that your quietness may be adorned with good
proportions and your bearing may appear something divine and
sacred. Be on your guard also against signs of arrogance, a haughty
bearing, a high head, a dainty and lofty footstep.

Let your speech be gentle to those you encounter, and your greetings kind; be modest towards women, and let your gaze be diverted to the ground. Be circumspect in all your talk, and return a serviceable answer, suiting your words to your hearers' needs, loud enough to be heard clearly, neither escaping the hearing of those present by being too slight nor going to excess with too great a noise. Take care never to speak what you have previously not weighed and deliberated; nor interject offhand your own words in the midst of another's; for you must listen and talk in turn, with set times for speech and for silence. Learn gladly and teach ungrudgingly; never hinder wisdom from others because of jealousy, nor stand aloof from instruction through false modesty.

Do all things unto the Lord, both deeds and words, and offer up to Christ all that is yours; and turn your soul frequently to God; and lean your thoughts on the might of Christ as if in some harbour by the divine light of the Saviour it were resting from all talk and traffic. And often by day impart your thoughts to men, but especially to God by night as well as by day; for let not much sleep prevail to hinder your prayers and hymns to God, for deep sleep is a rival of death.

Relax not the tension of your soul with feasting and licence in drink, but hold that to be sufficient which is needful for the body. And do not hasten early to meals before the time for dinner has arrived, but let your dinner be a loaf, and let all the fruits of the ground and of the trees be set before you; and go to your meal with equanimity, showing no sign of ravening gluttony. Be neither a flesh eater nor a lover of wine, when no ailment leads you to it as a remedy. But instead of delights that are in these things, choose the joys that are in divine words and hymns, joys with which you are abundantly furnished by the wisdom of God; and let heavenly meditation ever conduct you upwards to heaven.

And neglect the many anxious thoughts about the body by being confident in the hope towards God; because he will provide all necessary things for you in sufficiency, food to sustain life, covering for the body and protection against winter cold. For the whole earth and whatever it brings forth belongs to your King, and

God tends diligently, as his own members, the bodies of those who serve him, like his own shrines and temples.

Knowing this, equip your soul to be strong even in the face of disease; be of good courage as a man in the arena, bravest to withstand his conflicts with strength unmoved. Be not altogether crushed in soul by grief, whatever oppressive diseases torment you, or any other hardship befalls, but nobly withstand the conflicts with your understanding, even in the midst of your struggles rendering thanks to God. Have pity on those who are in distress, and ask for men the succour that comes from God; for he will grant grace to his friend when he asks, and will give aid for those in distress, wishing to make his power known to men, in the hope that, when they have come to full knowledge, they may return to God and enjoy eternal blessedness when the Son of God shall come and restore good things to his own.

6

The Inner Life of the Church

THE Church, as we have seen in the previous chapter, is constantly subjected to the temptation to compromise, and not only to compromise but even to capitulate, to surrender its values and ideals and accept those of the world in which it lives. Yet, so its members believe, it possesses the means to resist this temptation and to advance, if not entirely unscathed, at least not essentially corrupted, towards the consummation of its inheritance. These means comprise its supernatural endowment, i.e. the presence of the Holy Spirit and the practice of the spiritual life which he alone makes possible. Whatever influences may impinge upon it from outside, the all-important factor, which determines whether or not these influences may be recreatively assimilated to the enrichment of the Church as a whole, is the continuity of its contact with the divine and the preservation of its living relationship with its Founder who alone can ensure its enduring vitality. Consequently no account of the making of the Church can be deemed complete that does not lay stress on those factors which the Church itself considered and considers to be so important. It is indeed in the exercise of its inner life of prayer and worship that the Church is most truly itself and keeps open its life-lines to eternity.

This inner life is frequently said to have a twofold aspect, private and public; the former relating to the devotions of the individuals and the latter to the corporate acts of the whole community. But this distinction is somewhat artificial, for the single Christian does not cease to be a member of the Body of Christ even when he prays alone and the community, however great its cohesion, never ceases to be a unity of individual believers. This should be constantly borne in mind as a corrective to the ensuing account which for the sake of clarity will be described in this customary dual manner.

The example and precept of Jesus made it incumbent upon his followers to practise the life of prayer. Before all his great decisions he spent time in prayer—before the choice of the apostles or in the garden of Gethsemane—alone on a hill top or apart in a desert place. 'Ask, and it shall be given you,' he told his disciples, and when they complained of their failure to heal, he said: 'This kind can come out by nothing, save by prayer.'

The picture of the primitive community that may be derived from Acts shows that they had learned their lesson and so we find that the appointment of the Seven was in order that the apostles might 'continue steadfastly in prayer, and in the ministry of the word'. The Epistles recount the same story, being full of assurances by the writer of his prayers for his correspondents and requests that they in their turn will pray for him.

In this activity the Christian believed he was communing with God and thereby fostering an intensely personal relationship. He experienced a greater freedom in this than hitherto, for he was no longer a slave to sin but an adopted son and able, through the Spirit of adoption, to approach God as Father. His prayer was grounded in the Spirit who included him in the intercession of Christ at the right hand of the Father. A new way had been opened up to God and the Christian was eager to advance along it.

The literature of the second century does not differ in this particular from the New Testament writings. The necessity of prayer was self-evident except to a few whose knowledge of Greek philosophy led them to raise a subtle objection. These were the followers of a certain Prodicus, whom Origen sought to answer in his treatise on prayer (*c.* 236). They argued that since God has foreknowledge of all that will take place, everything that happens is predetermined and prayer is therefore useless. Origen replied that God's foreknowledge takes account of man's undoubted free will so that his over-all plan embraces man's free response; the free response of prayer therefore, which is foreknown but not predetermined, is a necessary part of the working out of the divine purpose. At the same time of course it should be noted that the Prodicians were working with a very narrow concept of prayer; they seem to have limited it exclusively to petition so that it consisted solely in asking God for certain gifts and services. They did not appreciate that prayer was not a means of changing God's mind but of subjecting the human will to his and that it involved also confession, praise, thanksgiving and intercession, thereby expressing the Godward direction of the whole of human life, hence Tertullian's words: 'Prayer is the wall of faith: her arms and missiles against the foe who keeps watch over us on all sides. And so, may we never walk unarmed.'

Yet despite the fact that within a period of fifty years three separate treatises were issued on prayer—by Tertullian, Origen and Cyprian—there was no science of prayer properly so-called. Advice was mainly of a simple and practical kind. So the faithful were told to make sure that they bore no malice to anyone before beginning to pray, to start by recollecting the presence of God, to seek to put aside all extraneous thoughts, banishing anger and whatever might disturb the tranquillity of their approach to the Father. They were reminded of the intimate connection between prayer and conduct, hence, according to Cyprian: 'we ought, beloved brethren, to remember and to know that when we call God Father, we ought to act as

God's children, so that in the measure in which we find pleasure in considering God as Father, he might also be able to find pleasure in us. Let us converse as temples of God, that it may be plain that God dwells in us.'

Regular and frequent prayer was also encouraged. 'Believers ought not to take food,' says Tertullian, 'nor go to the baths before interposing a prayer; for the refreshment and nourishment of the spirit are to be held prior to that of the flesh, and things heavenly prior to things earthly.' Similarly, when friends leave your house, they should not be dismissed without prayer.

Yet the Fathers were not only prepared to recommend, they were also concerned to regulate private prayer. In the *Didache* three times a day is prescribed. In the *Apostolic Tradition* seven hours of prayer are listed—as soon as one wakes; at the third, sixth and ninth hours; before sleep; at midnight and finally at cockcrow. Of these the first and the fifth would seem to have been adopted very early in imitation of Jewish practice: the second, third and fourth corresponded to the main divisions of the day in the Roman world which were Christianized by relating them to the events of Christ's Passion—at the third hour Christ was nailed to the Cross; at the sixth darkness came over the land and at the ninth his side was pierced with the lance. The origins of the final pair, midnight and cockcrow, are uncertain.

Several devotional practices were also connected with prayer, although not all the Fathers were prepared to condone them. Tertullian objected to those who first removed their cloaks in imitation of the pagans when approaching idols; he disliked also the washing of the hands before prayer, although Hippolytus was in favour of it. He rejected out of hand the sitting down on a bed immediately after prayer which some apparently regarded as necessary in view of a statement in the *Shepherd* of Hermas (120–40) to the effect that when he had prayed, he sat down on his bed. All Church leaders however considered that the most suitable posture for prayer was standing upright with arms outstretched in imitation of the Crucifixion, kneeling being reserved for confession of sin, with the face turned to the East, since, according to Clement, 'the dawn is an image of the day of birth, and from that point the light which has shone forth at first from the darkness increases, there has also dawned on those involved in darkness a day of the knowledge of truth'. Other later comments on this practice were those of Chrysostom who referred to its appropriateness since Christ is the 'Dayspring from high' and the 'Light of the World', of Hilary († 367) that Christians are looking for the Lord's return, since the coming of the Son of man will be like 'the lightning that cometh out of the East and shineth even unto the West', and of Basil that the soul is looking for its restoration to its ancient home in Paradise through Christ the Second Adam.

The sign of the Cross too was a frequent devotional action. 'In all our travels and movements,' says Tertullian, 'in all our coming in and going out, in putting on our shoes, at the bath, at the table, in lighting our candles, in lying down, in sitting down, whatever employment occupies us, we mark our forehead with the sign of the cross.' And from Hippolytus: 'seek always modestly to sign thy forehead; for this is the sign of his Passion, manifest and approved against the devil if so thou makest it from faith'.

Yet another feature of domestic piety was the ceremony of lighting the lamp, which eventually became part of the public worship of the Church under the name of the *Lucernarium*. In origin this derived from the Jewish custom of lighting and blessing a lamp at the evening meal which signified the beginning and ending of the Sabbath on Friday and Saturday evenings. An insertion, from an oriental source, in the *Apostolic Tradition*, provides some indication of the ideas expressed in this little service:

When evening has come and the bishop is present, the deacon shall bring in a lamp. Then the bishop, standing in the midst of the believers, before giving thanks, shall first give the salutation: 'The Lord be with you all.' And the people shall say: 'With thy spirit.' And the bishop shall say: 'Let us give thanks to the Lord.' And the people shall say: 'It is meet and right. Majesty, exaltation and glory are due to Him.' But they shall not say 'Lift up your hearts', for that belongs to the Eucharist. And he prays thus, saying: 'We give thee thanks, O God, because thou hast enlightened us by revealing the incorruptible light. So we, having finished the length of a day, and being come to the beginning of the night, satisfied with the light of the day that thou hast created for our satisfaction; and now, since by thy grace we lack not a light for the evening, we sanctify thee and we glorify thee. Through thine only Son our Lord Jesus Christ, through whom be to thee with him glory and might and honour with the Holy Spirit. 'And they shall all say: "Amen." '

Side by side with these practices we must also note, as features of the Church's inner life, Bible reading, fasting and alms-giving. The Bible of the early Church was at first the Septuagint, i.e. the Greek translation of our present Old Testament plus the Apocrypha. It was the custom, as in the Jewish synagogues, to read portions at the gatherings for worship both of this and of such Christian writings as were in circulation. This led to the inference that the latter was as authoritative as the former and so to the formation of a corpus of Christian Scriptures to be added to the corpus of Jewish Scriptures.

Each local church had its own collection and the question naturally arose: what shall be included in our canon or reading list? The answer was determined by a combination of three factors: first, whether or not the book had been written by an apostle or by the associate of an apostle; second, whether or not the book was accepted by the Church at large, and, third, whether or not its contents were generally edifying. By the latter half of the second century there was widespread agreement on the main contents of these lists. At the beginning of the fourth century Eusebius of Caesarea divided the New Testament writings into three classes: (1) acknowledged books, (2) disputed, (3) spurious. The unification of the first two categories produced the twenty-seven books of the New Testament as it is known today, and this combination appears for the first time in the Festal Letter of Athanasius for the year 367, and from then on received general approval.

It was these Old and New Testaments that contained for the Christian the title deeds of his faith and he was expected to read them assiduously. The illiterate would gather in groups to listen to one of the more educated brethren, the literate obtained such copies as they could, if not complete, then a portion of the Scriptures, for home study. 'Sit at home,' orders the *Didascalia*, 'and read the Law, and the Book of Kings, and the Prophets, and the Gospel which is the fulfilment of these.' Time and again we find the Fathers insisting on regular recourse to the record of revelation and Jerome's advice to a parent on the upbringing of her child is typical of the general viewpoint.

Let your child's treasures be not swords and armour, nor silk and gems, but manuscripts of the holy Scriptures; and in these let him think less of gilding and Babylonian parchment and arabesque patterns than of correctness and accurate punctuation. Let him begin by learning the Psalter, and then let him gather rules of life out of the Proverbs of Solomon. From Ecclesiastes let him gain the habit of despising the world and its vanities. Let him follow the example set by Job of virtue and patience. Then let him pass on to the Gospels, never to be put aside when once they have been taken in hand. Let him also drink in with a willing heart the Acts of the Apostles and the Epistles. As soon as he has enriched the storehouse of his mind with these treasures, let him learn by heart the prophets, the heptateuch, the books of Kings and of Chronicles, the rolls also of Ezra and Esther. When he has done all this, he may safely read the Song of Songs, but not before: for, were he to read it at the beginning, he would fail to perceive that though it is written in fleshly words it is a marriage song of a spiritual bride—and not understanding this he would suffer hurt from it. Let it be his daily task to bring you the flowers which he has culled from the Scriptures.

Another spiritual exercise upon which stress was laid was fasting. That Christians should fast followed logically from their acceptance of the authority of the Old Testament, in which it is described and repeatedly prescribed, and from their imitation of Christ who after his Baptism and before the opening of his public ministry fasted in the wilderness. Its basis lay in the Hebrew conception of human nature which regarded man as an ensouled body, i.e. as an indivisible whole. He might have a spiritual and a physical side to his being, but these were but two different ways of regarding the one totality. Hence physical and psychical react upon one another, and what the Christian does with his body is not indifferent as regards his spiritual health. Consequently fasting, or abstinence from food for a specific period of time, was as much a spiritual as a physical discipline. By it the Christian was enabled to practise mortification and self-denial; it was an exercise in self-control; it restrained the fleshly appetites and was a check to self-indulgence. Moreover just as a feast is a sign of rejoicing, so a fast is a sign of mourning and is therefore a necessary element in penitential discipline. To Tertullian it was 'a work of reverential awe' and his view was shared by the Church at large.

From the second century Wednesdays and Fridays were observed as weekly fasts, i.e. days on which food was not partaken before three o'clock in the afternoon. The choice of these two days would seem to have been determined by opposition to the Jewish custom of fasting on Mondays and Thursdays, and the Christian fasts were given a Gospel reference insofar as the Wednesday was connected with the betrayal of Christ and the Friday with his Crucifixion. To these two was given the title 'Station-days', which was derived from the Latin word *statio* meaning a picket or military guard. So the idea was expressed that Christians by fasting were standing 'on watch' or keeping 'guard duty' by preparing themselves to welcome the Lord at his second coming. Initially these fasts were quite voluntary, although a bishop might order the observance of special days for a specific reason. As a form of spiritual preparation fasting also came to be observed before Easter and by catechumens before their baptism.

Closely linked with fasting was the further practice of almsgiving. Indeed in the *Shepherd* of Hermas it is stated:

in the day on which you fast you will taste nothing but bread and water; and having reckoned up the price of the dishes of that day which you intended to have eaten, you will give it to a widow, or an orphan, or to some person in want, and thus you will exhibit humility of mind, so that he who has received benefit from your humility may fill his own soul, and pray for you to the Lord.

Tertullian witnesses to the same intention when he refers to fasting 'for the special purpose of collecting contributions of alms'. Thus the different elements in the devotional life of the individual were seen to form part of a coherent whole, being interdependent, and hence Cyprian's assertion: 'our prayers and fastings are of less avail, unless they are aided by almsgiving'.

The basic principles of Christian charity are enunciated in the New Testament; first, by Christ himself in the words: 'Inasmuch as ye did it unto one of these my brethren, even these least, ye did it unto me.' Cyprian, in his treatise on almsgiving, shows his understanding of this by his statement:

'what is given to the poor and needy is given to Christ'. The second principle was framed, less succinctly, by Paul. In II Corinthians he exhorted his readers to give liberally to the collection for the Jerusalem community and he said: 'Ye know the grace of our Lord Jesus Christ, that, though he was rich, yet for your sakes he became poor, that ye through his poverty might become rich.' This is not just an illustration of the need for charity but the very foundation of Christian giving. The response of the Christian in gratitude for his Lord's self-impoverishment must be self-giving, for giving to the believer is giving to Christ who gave himself for us.

The extent of Christian giving in the early centuries was quite phenomenal, and the objects of this charity have been conveniently summarized for us by Tertullian:

Though we have our treasure-chest, it is not made up of fees, as though we contracted for our worship. On the monthly collection day, if he likes, each puts in a small donation; but only if it be his pleasure, and only if he be able; for there is no compulsion; all is voluntary. These gifts are, as it were, the deposits of piety. For they are not expended upon feasts and drinking-bouts and eating-houses, but to support and bury poor people, to supply the wants of boys and girls destitute of means and parents, and of old persons confined to the house; such too as have suffered shipwreck; and if there happen to be any in the mines, or banished to the islands, or shut up in the prisons, for nothing but their fidelity to the cause of God's Church, they become the nurslings of their confession.

So impressive was the flow of alms that even the heathen said of Christians, 'See how they love one another,' and Julian the Apostate bore grudging witness by urging his pagan church to imitate it. Reference has already been made to the widows supported by the Christian community and to the vast number of poor assisted at Constantinople, and one further example must suffice to illustrate this intense activity. In 253 hordes of robbers invaded Numidia and carried off many Christians; Cyprian, at Carthage, immediately instituted a collection and forwarded the by no means inconsiderable proceeds to the bishops for the redemption of the captives and the relief of those who had suffered.

With the Peace of the Church the volume of charity by no means diminished; indeed, freed from persecution, Christianity could display its natural tendencies without danger or restriction. Hence we hear of hospitals for sick, built, for example, by Basil at Caesarea or by Chrysostom at Constantinople or Paulinus at Nola. We hear of houses for foundlings, the aged and the poor, of guest-houses for travellers, of support by rich churches for the less materially favoured ones, of the care of the indigent needing burial and of assistance for those visited by such calamities as the plague.

Here was one way, so the Christian believed, whereby he could both serve and imitate his Master. And here too, according to the teaching of certain Fathers, was a remedy for sin. 'By almsgiving,' says Cyprian, 'we may wash away whatever foulness we contract subsequent to Baptism.' It was this conception of charity, tinged sometimes with the motive of self-regard, which was to play such a vital part in the Middle Ages in the erection of monastic houses, cathedrals, schools, etc.

The forms of the inner life of the Church that we have just examined were not and could not be so insulated that they were immune to outside pressure. In the fourth century with the large influx of nominal Christians, to which attention has already been drawn repeatedly, this pressure increased to such an extent that the health and purity of the Church's inner life was seriously threatened. How critical the situation was may be gauged from the many despairing pronouncements on the Church's condition at this period, as witness these words of Basil:

The doctrines of the Fathers are despised, the speculations of innovators hold sway in the Church . . . the wisdom of this world has the place of honour having dispossessed the boasting of the Cross. The shepherds are driven out; in their place grievous wolves are brought in which harry the flock. Houses of prayer have none to assemble in them; the deserts are full of mourners.

The last phrase of this statement has reference to the monks who, at the time when this letter was written, already formed a great multitude devoted exclusively to spiritual exercise in the deserts of Egypt and Syria. Indeed in its origins the monastic movement was primarily a protest against the secularization of the Church, against a compromise with the world which seemed to be being forced upon it by the incursion of time-servers and half-converted pagans. The Church's inner life was at stake; that it was preserved depended largely upon the ardour of the monks who by their refusal to compromise saved and perpetuated the Christian ideal of total surrender to God. Nevertheless fourth-century monasticism was not without its roots in the Christian past. Already in the second century groups of virgins and ascetics had existed within the different congregations, their distinction becoming more apparent as the latter increased in size. All that was required to transform them into monks and nuns proper was complete withdrawal from the congregation accompanied by the formulation of a common rule and discipline. The Peace of the Church only served to accentuate their already existing distinction and to provide a further compelling reason for separation.

The desert fathers fled therefore not so much from the world as from the world in the Church. There were of course other influences at work, e.g. the persecutions had driven many into the desert where they discovered it possible to practise piety unhampered by the temptations of life in a pagan environment; again the economic situation, with the ever increasing burden of taxation, led many to forsake the world which cost so much, but the main factor was the lowering of the ideal of Christian perfection inseparable from mass conversion. This meant that monasticism was at first, as it were, outside the Church—or at least outside the organized community life of the Church—since it was as much a flight from the Church as from the world. Further this involved the hostility of those in authority in the Church and for many years there were more bishops persecuting the monks and attempting to stamp out the movement than there were supporting it. But the high ideal of renunciation, the recognition both that Christ's teaching, at least from one aspect, was essentially ascetic and that the monks were the true heirs of the revered martyrs inasmuch as they embraced the same ideal of self-surrender, together with the abundant fruits of holiness produced by their austere and simple lives, brought about its speedy acceptance. When leaders such as Athanasius, Basil, Chrysostom, Jerome and Augustine gave them their whole-hearted support and sang their praises, there was little doubt that the Church as a whole would soon recognize the worth of these 'athletes of God'.

Since monasticism was initially a protest of individuals, it assumed at its beginnings an essentially individualistic character: the first monks were hermits. Such indeed at first was the great Antony who is usually regarded as the founder of Christian monasticism.

Antony was born about 251 in the village of Coma in Middle Egypt of well-to-do Christian parents. Shortly after their death, when he was only eighteen years old, he gave away all his inheritance, in response to the Gospel message 'Sell all that thou hast', and put himself under the tutelage of an old ascetic who lived on the outskirts of his village; there he worked with his hands, prayed and read the Bible. For thirty-five years, part of which time he lived in a tomb and part in a disused castle, he devoted himself to ascetic practices until his reputation for sanctity attracted such crowds that, seeking greater solitude, he fled further into the desert. Many however followed him and, building cells near his own, lived a semi-eremitical life under his guidance. Apart from two visits to Alexandria, one in 311 to strengthen those suffering persecution and one shortly before his death to oppose the Arians, he remained in comparative seclusion, dying on January 17th, 356. This semi-eremitical life, the first of the two types of Egyptian monasticism, continued to flourish at Pispir, where Antony had lived in the castle, but its main centre was in the desert of Nitria, with that of Scete a close second.

Nitrian monasticism was founded by Amoun, between 320 and 330, and by the end of the fourth century it numbered five thousand adherents. The colony at Scete was established by Macarius the Egyptian, a disciple of Antony, who settled there c. 330 at the age of thirty. These monks lived under no common discipline, but following their own individual rule. They had separate cells where they worked at palm mats, using a little of the money from their sale for their meagre diet and distributing the rest to the poor. They met together on Saturdays and Sundays for the Eucharist, returning forthwith to their solitude, to their prayers, their learning of the Scriptures and their manual labour.

The second type of Egyptian monasticism and that which was destined to prevail widely was cenobitism, a title composed of two Greek words *koinos* and *bios* meaning common life, i.e. it involved living according to ascetic principles within an organized community. Here the pioneer was Pachomius. He was born c. 292 of pagan parents in the Upper Thebaid. After service in the army, he was converted to Christianity and joined himself to a hermit named Palamon with whom he lived for seven years. In 323 Pachomius settled at Tabennesis and within a short time he had around him some hundred or so followers whom he proceeded to organize into a community with a common rule of life. His system spread with such rapidity that by the time of his death in 346 he had under his control nine monasteries for men and two for women, and by the end of the century there were over seven thousand Pachomian monks.

Another great figure of Egyptian monastic history was Schenoudi, who was born c. 333–4. As a young boy he went to live with his uncle Bgoul, the head of the White Monastery, where the rule was a stricter form of that of Pachomius. Schenoudi succeeded his uncle d. 383 and continued as head until his death some eighty three years later. His monastery was essentially a Coptic institution where the Sahidic dialect was in use. He seems to have attempted to combine the cenobitical and eremitical as he was accustomed to depart with some of his monks to cells in the desert from time to time.

The visits of pilgrims to Egypt, the popularity of Athanasius' life of Antony, together with the same general causes that operated to originate monasticism, led to its adoption in countries other than that of its birth. In Palestine Hilarion was the prime instigator. Born c. 291 at Gaza, he was sent by his pagan parents to Alexandria to be educated. There he was converted, visited Antony and, returning home, practised the ascetic life. He soon became the centre of much attraction and founded several monasteries. Traditionally, monasticism is said to have been introduced into Mesopotamia by Eugenius, a disciple of Pachomius, but no historical truth can be attributed to this legend. It should be noticed however that whereas the tendency in Egypt was to abandon the eremitical life in favour of cenobitism, in Mesopotamia and Syria the opposite bias was at work, producing a series of astonishing figures who surpassed the Egyptians in their self-imposed austerities culminating in such a man as Simeon Stylites who spent the major part of his life on the top of a pillar.

It was Eustathius of Sebaste (born c. 300) who introduced

monasticism into the districts of Cappadocia and Pontus, but his chief importance lies in his influence on Basil. Born at Caesarea in Cappadocia, one of ten children, Basil was brought up as a Christian. At first he intended to embrace the career of a rhetorician, but eventually decided to devote himself to the ascetic life. In 357 he went on a journey through Syria and Egypt in order to familiarize himself with monastic ideals and practice at first hand.

I admired [he reported] their continence in living and their endurance in toil. I was amazed at their persistence in prayer and their triumphing over sleep. Subdued by no natural necessity, ever keeping their souls' purpose high and free, they never yielded to the body; always, as though living in a flesh that was not theirs, they showed in very deed what it is to sojourn for a while in this life, and what it is to have one's citizenship and home in heaven. All this moved my admiration. I called these men's lives blessed, in that they did indeed show that they 'bear about in their body the dying of Jesus'. And I prayed that I too, as far as in me lay, might imitate them.

Returning home, Basil sold his possessions and retired to Pontus; there he gathered disciples, including Gregory of Nazianzus, and organized his first monastery. It was indeed Basil who was the father of Greek monasticism, and the rules which he framed became the norm throughout the Greek Church. He was opposed to the eremitical life and laid his entire emphasis upon the community. Although indebted to Pachomius, he went beyond him in refusing to allow any personal idiosyncrasies to interfere with the life of the monastery; nor would he permit excesses of austerity, saying that they made a man unfit for work, which was more important than fasting.

So far we have been concerned exclusively with Eastern monasticism, and it is now time to consider its development in the West. Here Athanasius played a leading part. In 341 he came, in exile, to Italy accompanied by two Egyptian monks, and there he remained for several years, thus having ample time to inspire people with the example of the ascetic life. Details of its further immediate advance are not plentiful, but about 360 a small book was published, entitled *The Conferences of Zacchaeus and Apollonius*, possibly written by Firmicus Maternus, which is interesting as being both an apologetic for the movement against its detractors and evidence of its growing popularity. Yet even by 382, when Jerome came to stay in Rome, there was little organized cenobitic life. Jerome, who was later to found a monastery at Bethlehem and there produce a monument to his lasting fame in the form of the translation of the Bible known as the Vulgate, became the centre of a group of devout ladies meeting in the house of a certain Marcella on the Aventine Hill. They devoted their time to talking of holy things, to the study of the Scriptures and to the reading of psalms, and Jerome acted as their spiritual director, thus giving by his precept and example a further impetus to the ascetic movement. Soon monasteries were appearing in northern and central Italy, amongst which notice should be taken of that of Eusebius of Vercelli where the clerical and monastic states were combined.

A similar combination is to be found later in North Africa where Augustine was the prime mover. After his baptism by Ambrose at Milan in 387, he returned to Tagaste and there gathered about him a group of men who were prepared to give up all their worldly goods. When later he became bishop of Hippo he established a monastery where he lived together with his clergy. Many laity were attracted and from these Augustine recruited further members for the ranks of his clergy. The guidance that he gave this community and others that sprang up in imitation of it was contained in his *Letter 211*. The relevant section of this was detached and circulated as a Rule which was widely used in the Middle Ages and served as the basis for the constitutions of several religious orders, some being still in existence at the present day.

The first monastery in Gaul would seem to have been that of Martin near Poitiers c. 360, and when he became bishop of Tours in 372 he established another close to the city at Marmoutiers. There he gathered eighty monks who lived in caves and huts, met only for services and meals and fasted rigorously. Work amongst them was discouraged, apart from the transcription of manuscripts, and in many respects this was a close imitation of the simple Antonian monasticism in Egypt. The beginning of the fifth century saw the inauguration of the movement in Provence by Honoratus on the island of Lérins, just off Cannes. The life there was a mixture of the eremitical and cenobitic, and Lérins became a centre of Christian thought, supplying the Church in Gaul with a series of great bishops for many generations.

By the year 430 the monastic movement was well under way, but more important than its external history, which has just been sketched, was its inner spirit and ethos. This was given very clear expression by John Cassian. He was born c. 360 in Scythia, the district around the Danube Delta. Well educated by pious Christian parents, he forsook the world at an early age and together with his close friend Germanus entered a monastery at Bethlehem, which, as he tells us himself, 'was at no great distance from the cave in which our Lord vouchsafed to be born of a Virgin'. After several years, seeking to make further progress in the ascetic life, the two friends journeyed to Egypt where they stayed from 386 to 399, visiting the main centres. Cassian then went to Constantinople, where he was made deacon by John Chrysostom and, with Germanus, was placed in charge of the treasury, the only part of the cathedral which escaped destruction in the great fire of 404. The following year, after Chrysostom's disgrace and exile, Cassian went to Rome with the letter from those who supported the bishop, and there he was ordained priest. About 415 he settled at Marseilles where he founded two monasteries —the one for men, built over the tomb of Victor, a martyr in the Diocletian persecution, the other for women. Here he wrote his two works on the monastic vocation: the *Institutes* in 425, which he describes as concerned with 'what belongs to the outer man and the customs of the Cenobia', i.e. the life and system of a monastery, and the *Conferences*, 426, whose subject was 'the training of the inner man and the perfection of the heart'. In the former he includes an address to one who has just entered upon the noviciate and here in a short compass is the essence of the monastic calling:

You ought in the first instance to learn the actual reason for the renunciation of the world. Renunciation is nothing but the evidence of the cross and of mortification. And so you must know that today you are dead to this world, and that, as the apostle says, you are crucified to this world and this world to you. Consider, therefore, the demands of the cross under the sign of which you ought henceforth to live in this life; because *you* no longer live, but *he* lives in you who was crucified for you. We must therefore pass our time in this life in that fashion and form in which he was crucified for us on the cross so that we may have all our wishes and desires not subservient to our own lusts but fastened to his mortification. For so shall we fulfil the command of the Lord which says: 'He that taketh not up his cross and followeth me is not worthy of me.' But perhaps you will say: How can a man carry his cross continually? Or, how can anyone who is alive be crucified? Hear briefly how this is.

The fear of the Lord is our cross. As then one who is crucified no longer has the power of moving or turning his limbs in any direction, so we also ought to affix our wishes and desires—not in accordance with what is pleasant and delightful to us now—but in accordance with the law of the Lord, where it constrains us. For in this way we can have all our desires and carnal affections mortified.

Take heed to continue even to the end in that state of naked-
ness of which you made profession in the sight of God and of his
angels. For not he who begins these things, but he who endures in
them to the end shall be saved. The beginning of our salvation and
the safeguard of it is the fear of the Lord. For through this those
who are trained in the way of perfection can gain a start in conversion as well as purification from vices and security in virtue. And
when this has gained an entrance into a man's heart it produces a
contempt of things and begets a forgetfulness of kinsfolk and a
horror of the world itself. But by contempt for the loss of all
possessions humility is gained.

That you may the more easily arrive at this, you must observe
three things. As the Psalmist says: 'I was like a deaf man and heard
not, and as one that is dumb who doth not open his mouth; and I
became as a man that heareth not, and in whose mouth there are no
reproofs.' So you also should walk as one that is deaf and blind.
You should be like a blind man and not see any of those things
which you find to be unedifying. If you hear anyone disobedient or
disparaging another, you should not be led astray by such example
to imitate him, but 'like a deaf man', as if you had never heard it,
you should pass it all by. If insults are offered to you or wrong,
done, be immovable, and as far as answer in retaliation is concerned
be silent 'as one that is dumb'.

But cultivate above everything else this fourth thing which
adorns and graces the three things of which I have just spoken;
namely, make yourself, as the apostle says, a fool in this world that
you may become wise, exercising no judgement of your own on
any of those matters that are commanded you, but always showing
obedience, judging that alone to be holy which is God's law or the
decision of your superiors declares to be such. For built upon such a
system of instruction, you may continue for ever under this
discipline, and not fall away from this monastery in consequence of
any temptations or devices of the enemy.

There is little gainsaying the fact that these words present
a concept of spirituality which differs in its emphases from
that of the first generations of Christians. In New Testament

times the Christian life was not conceived primarily in terms of progress towards a goal because it was believed that the goal had already in large measure been reached through the action of God in Christ. Having died to sin, the believer belonged to a holy community; he was not a member of a school for sinners but of a society of saints. The Age to Come had dawned; the consummation would not be long delayed. The fading of the eschatological hope however and the recognition that the principle of sin, though it had received a mortal blow, was still active in its death throes, together with the influence of semi-Stoic ideas of existence as an advance or progress, led the Alexandrian Fathers to think of the Christian life as a training ground for souls. Though even here it should be noted that their work was not without its biblical basis since Paul himself had affirmed: 'Not that I have already obtained, or am already made perfect: but I press on . . . toward the goal unto the prize of the high calling of God in Christ Jesus.'

When the world pressed into the Church in the fourth century, ideas of schooling and discipline were already to hand for development to meet the new and serious situation of a watered-down Christianity. Clement had begun to think of God rather as a goal than as a present possession and Origen had already worked out the main features of an ascetical system in his quest for perfection. It was indeed the teaching of these two, developed by the desert Fathers, that led to the formulation of a science of the spiritual life which had become a practical necessity in view of the condition of the Church described above. The key figure in this development was Evagrius.

Evagrius was a citizen of Ibora in Pontus and after ordination to a readership by Basil and to the diaconate by Gregory of Nazianzus he became archdeacon of Constantinople and attended the council of 381. He eventually embraced the monastic life and withdrew to Cellia, north of Nitria, where he lived for fourteen years until his death in 399. In his writings he defined the goal of the Christian life and the means to attain it. He described the way of prayer; he analysed the virtues and the vices; he classified evil and laid the foundation of the later concept of the seven deadly sins; he gave advice on how to overcome temptation; he saw the Christian life as the ascending of a ladder with its several rungs clearly labelled. His Origenist spirituality was the main source of John Cassian's teaching, and eventually, through the work of Benedict, became the accepted norm of the Western Church. Benedict indeed, who was the principal architect of mediaeval monasticism, built with care and acumen upon the labour of his predecessors.

Born c. 480 at Nursia, Benedict spent his early years in Rome and then, after a time as a hermit in the district of Subiaco, eventually established a monastery on Monte Cassino, some eighty miles to the south of the capital, and remained there as abbot until his death in the middle decades of the sixth century. In Benedict Western monasticism found its great organiser and legislator. The tendency towards codification, which we have already noted as a characteristic of this period with its collection of canons, e.g. that of Dionysius Exiguus, making up the law of the Church, found expression in the Rule which Benedict intended not only for his own community but as a model for general imitation. In this work counsel was replaced by command, generalization by detailed direction, and exhortation by administrative procedure to preserve and inculcate the ideal. Benedict expected his monks to read their Cassian, but he did not rest content with this and sought to foster sanctity by habit-forming rules approved and maintained by authority. He devised a constitution for the monastery which left no doubt as to who was in authority and he endeavoured to avoid failure by legislating for every possible situation. In contrast with the individualism of the hermits and the large measure of personal preference allowed by Pachomius, Benedict, like Basil, legislated for a community life free from excesses. The monks were to live as a family under the government of the abbot to whom they were to promise utter obedience. They were to observe poverty, chastity and stability, i.e. they were not to pass from house to house but remain within the confines of their own. They had to share in the agricultural and domestic work, read, and learn the psalms. Their time-table was regulated by the performance of the divine office, i.e. the recital of the hours of prayer—Vigils at 2 a.m., Lauds at dawn, Prime at six, Terce at nine, Sext at noon, None at four, Vespers at four-thirty and Compline at six. This was the system, partly through its intrinsic merit and partly through the influence of such men as Gregory the Great, that was gradually adopted throughout Europe, replacing even the vigorous Celtic monasticism which had flourished in comparative isolation on the extreme confines of the Western empire.

If the first monks, with their incredible austerities, tend to elicit a horrified admiration at their strong personal love for Christ and their eagerness to surrender all for his sake, their later followers in the West, moulded by the judicious counsel of a Cassian and a Benedict, were remarkable for their balanced spirituality. No one can read their very abundant literary remains without being struck by their humour and their sanctified common sense. 'To drink wine with reason,' wrote Palladius in the preface to his *Lausiac History*, 'is better than to drink water with pride.' 'Remember,' counselled Cassian, 'a reasonable supply of food partaken daily with moderation is better than severe and long fasts at intervals.' If within their cells they seem to have lived a sheltered life they came, through the knowledge of their own temptations and weaknesses, to an understanding of human nature which was nothing if not profound, and the helps they devised for the preservation of virtue and the casting out of sin have features of enduring value. So, for example, the advice of Cassian to his

monks at Marseilles on the subject of prayer has lost nothing
through the passage of time:

Whatever our mind has been thinking of before the hour of
prayer is sure to occur to us while we are praying, through the
activity of the memory. Wherefore what we want to find ourselves
like while we are praying, that we ought to prepare ourselves to be
before the time of prayer. For the mind in prayer is formed by its
previous condition, and when we are applying ourselves to prayer
the images of the same actions and words and thoughts will dance
before our eyes.

That the inner life of the Church was not irreparably corrupted was due in no small measure to these 'athletes of God'.
Moreover, relatively secure and self-supporting within their
monasteries, each with its well, its mill and its garden, they
were able to preserve a pattern of life and learning throughout
the period of economic anarchy which began with the fall of
the Roman Empire. With their transcriptions and their libra-
ries they guarded the wisdom of their forefathers and thus
enabled the gradual building up of a new culture. With their
rigorous training and discipline, they produced the men who
were to be the missionaries, schoolmasters, editors of the
Fathers, abbots and statesmen of the Middle Ages. If at times
they needed a Benedict of Aniane or a Bernard of Clairvaux
to recall them to the ideals of their founders, they were an in-
dispensable element in the long process of the making of the
Church.

7

The Inner Life of the Church (*continued*)

PERHAPS the greatest weakness of the earliest monks, the solitaries of the desert, was their excessive individualism—though this was, in large measure, forced upon them by the circumstances of the time—for a balanced Christian spirituality requires not only personal private devotion but also active participation in the corporate life of the Church. This aspect of the Church's inner life is to be found in its acts of public worship and its sacraments.

Worship involves the recognition of God's majesty and the acknowledgement of his sovereignty; it means therefore reverent homage issuing in the adoration of and devotion to the personal God. Worship is further man's response to the gracious activity of God—a response which, to the Christian, has already been made by Christ himself in his humanity, and consequently all Christian worship is made through him, being rendered possible here and now by the divine presence in the person of the Holy Spirit. From such a definition it becomes plain that worship is not or should not be just one element among many in the life of believers; it is rather an attitude and an orientation which should characterize the whole of it. For this reason we do not find in the New Testament any essential distinction between worship and daily life—man's existence is not divided into two areas, one where Christ is honoured and the other where man is more or less independent.

There are not two levels, the sacred and the secular, since both are one through the God-man. Everything stands under his supreme Lordship. This did not mean however that the first Christians did not engage in what may be termed specific acts of worship, but that they did so depended upon their acceptance of the sacramental principle, which derived primarily from their understanding of Christ.

Christian belief as to the nature of Christ, implicit from the outset but only made explicit after centuries of debate, was that he was perfect God and perfect man in one person. As such he was obviously unique, but at the same time he was representative of the true relation of the whole of mankind to God. The Sacraments similarly take the particular—a specific quantity of water in baptism or a particular piece of bread and a drop of wine in the Eucharist—in order to represent the true relation of the whole to God and to be the means whereby this relation is more effectively realized. Thus the relation of specific acts of worship to life is that of the particular to the universal, that through the former the whole might be sanctified and recognized as subject to the divine sovereignty. Without this thankful response in public acts of worship to God's initiative man is in constant danger of forgetting that all his life is to be an obedient service.

The sacramental principle is based further upon the Christian understanding of man which itself rests upon the Hebrew conception. To the Hebrew, man has not a body, he *is* a body. There is no rigid distinction between the physical and the spiritual because body and soul are so intimately united that they cannot be distinguished; indeed they are more than united, for the body is regarded as the soul in its outward form. Man in his totality therefore is not a discarnate spirit but a spiritual-corporal unity. It was precisely because of this that God became man, for Christ came not to save the spiritual side of human nature but the whole of man. God in Christ therefore met man at man's level, i.e. at the level of his corporal existence, and God continues to meet man, so Christians believe, at this same level when such physical entities as bread and wine become the instruments of communion. In the essential corporate acts of the Church, therefore, we find this concern for the material, just as we have already noted in connexion with the practice of fasting. So at baptism, which took place normally in the presence of the entire local congregation, the candidates were washed in a river or a lake or even in the sea, depending upon which was conveniently to hand; oil was smeared upon them, which could equally have been used for cooking or lighting a lamp, and hands were laid on their heads, hands hardened with the making of tents or the hauling of nets. Man in all the elemental contingencies of his earthly destiny was thereby encountering the divine.

It is time now to turn from general principles to a more detailed account of early Christian worship and to describe first that rite of incorporation into the Church to which allusion has just been made, viz. baptism. The origin of baptism lay partly in the imitation of Jesus in his submission to the baptism of John and partly in that of Jewish proselyte baptism whereby converts to Judaism were purified from their previous contamination as Gentiles. In the Apostolic Age baptism could take place at any time and in any place. Whether or not it normally included the laying on of hands—the later rite of Confirmation—is debatable, but when one remembers that to the Jews this action was a sign of identification it is, to say the least, probable since baptism did identify the candidate with the community. Two other features of the ceremonial for which there is clear evidence in the second century are the anointing of the candidates and the clothing of them in white garments to symbolize their new-born purity. It has been argued that references to unction in a baptismal context in the New Testament and to the putting on of Christ indicate that these two practices derived from the earliest times. It is how-ever difficult to be certain of this, since while the passages in question may reflect current practice, equally they may be only the basis from which the later unambiguously attested practices developed. There is slight evidence that baptism did include a liturgical question—What doth hinder me from being baptized?—together with a short confession of Christ. That total immersion too was the primitive custom is a commonly held opinion, but it is doubtful if this was always feasible and very soon affusion became quite normal.

The great majority of converts were of course adults and whether or not children were included is uncertain. There is mention of 'households' being accepted which may or may not have involved infants, but when some wanted even the dead to be baptized it is unlikely that they would have been content to leave out their offspring. By the end of the second century it was quite widely practised, and Tertullian objected to it on the grounds that the age of innocence does not need to hurry to the remission of sins. Cyprian, in the middle of the third century, supported it, condemning those who would delay it to the eighth day by analogy with circumcision. A century later Gregory of Nazianzus expressed a preference for delaying until the child was at least three years old and had some rational understanding, but by the time of Augustine it was universal.

If at first all those who accepted Jesus as Lord were wel-comed, the need for some form of preparatory training soon became apparent and so there came into existence what is known as the catechumenate, i.e. a group of those undergoing instruction. Indeed much of the ethical teaching common to the New Testament epistles would appear to derive from a primitive Christian catechism used for these candidates and soon a careful system had been devised. A probationary period of three years was widely required towards the end of which those who had persevered were carefully examined or scrutinized, their sponsors questioned and their names inscribed on the church register. A period of intensive teaching followed, corresponding later to the season of Lent, involving repeated exorcisms, the delivery of the Creed and a series of homilies expounding the faith but avoiding all explanation of baptism itself and of the Eucharist. This reticence, known as the *disciplina arcani*, was due to motives of reverence and the belief that the disclosure of such mysteries to the uninitiated would be the betrayal of a sacred trust. Corresponding to the development of this system was an elaboration in the rites of baptism itself which may be seen already advanced in the *Apostolic Tradition*.

At the hour when the cock crows (on Sunday morning) they shall first pray over the water. When they come to the water, let the water be pure and flowing. And they shall put off their clothes. And they shall baptize the little children first. And if they can answer for themselves, let them answer. But if they cannot, let their parents answer or someone from their family. And next they shall baptize the grown men; and last the women, who shall have loosed their hair and laid aside the gold ornaments. Let no one go down to the water having any alien object with them.

And at the time determined for baptizing the bishop shall give thanks over the oil and put it into a vessel and it is called the Oil of Thanksgiving. And he shall take also another oil and exorcize over it, and it is called Oil of Exorcism. And let a deacon carry the Oil of Exorcism and stand on the left hand of the presbyter who will do the anointing. And another deacon shall take the Oil of Thanksgiving and stand on the right hand.

And when the presbyter takes hold of each one of those who are to be baptized, let him bid him renounce, saying: I renounce thee, Satan, and all thy service and all thy works. And when he has said this, let him anoint him with the Oil of Exorcism, saying: Let all evil spirits depart far from thee.

Then after these things let him give him over to the presbyter who stands at the water; and let them stand in the water naked. And let a deacon likewise go down with him into the water.

And when he goes down into the water, let him who baptizes lay a hand on him saying thus: Dost thou believe in God the Father Almighty? And he who is being baptized shall say: I believe. Let him forthwith baptize him once, having his hand laid upon his head. And after this let him say: Dost thou believe in Christ Jesus, the Son of God, Who was born of Holy Spirit and the Virgin Mary, Who was crucified in the days of Pontius Pilate, and died, and rose the third day living from the dead, And ascended into heaven, And sat down at the right hand of the Father, And will come to judge the living and the dead? And when he says: I believe, let him baptize him the second time. And again let him say: Dost thou believe in the Holy Spirit in the Holy Church, And the resurrection of the flesh? And he who is being baptized shall say: I believe. And so let him baptize him the third time.

And afterwards when he comes up, he shall be anointed by the presbyters with the Oil of Thanksgiving, saying: I anoint thee with holy oil in the Name of Jesus Christ. And each one drying himself, they shall now put on their clothes and after this let them be together in the assembly.

And the bishop shall lay his hand upon them invoking and saying: O Lord God, who didst count these worthy of deserving the forgiveness of sins by the laver of regeneration, make them worthy to be filled with thy Holy Spirit and send upon them thy grace, that they may serve thee according to thy will; to thee the glory, to the Father and to the Son with the Holy Spirit in the Holy Church, both now and ever and world without end. Amen.

After this, bringing the consecrated oil, and laying his hand on his head, he shall say: I anoint thee with holy oil in God the Father Almighty and Christ Jesus and the Holy Spirit. And sealing him on the forehead he shall give him the kiss and say: The Lord be with you. And he who has been sealed shall say: And with thy spirit. And so shall he do to each one in turn.

The rite at Jerusalem, some one hundred and fifty years later, has many of the same features but with certain local and

Eastern differences. The candidates assembled in the vestibule of the baptistery and there, facing the West (the region of darkness), they stretched out their hands and said: I renounce thee, Satan, and all thy works, and all thy pomp, and all thy worship. Then turning to the East (the region of light) they were told to say: I believe in the Father and in the Son and in the Holy Spirit, and in one Baptism of repentance. They then removed their clothes, imitating the stripping of Christ naked on the cross, and moved into the inner chamber for anointing from head to foot with exorcized oil. Next they approached the font singly, answered the interrogation as to belief in Father, Son and Spirit, and descended three times into the water, symbolizing the three days' burial of Christ. Unction followed, first on the forehead that they might be delivered from shame; then on the ears that they might be quick to hear divine mysteries; next on the nostrils that they might say: 'We are to God a sweet savour of Christ, in them that are saved'; finally on the breast that having put on the breast-plate of righteousness they might stand against the wiles of the devil. Dressed once again, but now in white robes, they processed to the church for their first Eucharist to the chanting of the psalm: 'Blessed are they whose iniquities are forgiven, and whose sins are covered.'

The Milanese rite, described by Ambrose in the course of commenting upon it, has other interesting additions. Baptism, as was now general, took place on Easter Eve and began with the *Effeta* or 'opening of the ears'. This was performed by touching the ears and the nostrils, based upon Jesus' healing of the deaf and dumb man, and was intended to signify the opening of the faculties to the fruitful reception of the Sacraments. Unction at the font came next, being the anointing as 'Christ's athlete, about to wrestle in the fight of this world'. Then after the renunciations, and the consecration of the font by the bishop, the candidate descended into the water, made his profession and was immersed three times. Unction of the head followed, whereby he was associated in the priesthood of all believers, and then the washing of the feet, a lesson in humility following Jesus' action at the Last Supper. The vesting in white robes preceded the 'spiritual seal', which was connected with the sevenfold gift of the Spirit, and then the proceedings were completed by a procession to the altar.

Of equal importance as a knowledge of the external details of the rite is an understanding of the meaning ascribed to it. Baptism may be considered from many aspects which determine the expression of its meaning; these different aspects are themselves determined by the particular conception of the Church which dominates, consciously or subconsciously, the mind of the writer. Thus if the idea of the Church as the Messianic Community or the New Israel is uppermost, then baptism is the means of initiation into it; it is spiritual circumcision whereby the candidate is marked and accepted as a member of the Chosen People. So according to Justin: 'We, who approach God through Christ, have received not carnal but spiritual circumcision . . . and we have received it through Baptism.' If the Church is being regarded as the Temple of the Divine Presence, then baptism is the means of bringing the individual into that Presence in the person of the Holy Spirit. So, according to the epistle to the Hebrews, Christians are 'partakers', i.e. sharers or partners, in the Holy Spirit. Again, if the Church is the Body of Christ, it is through baptism that the catechumen is incorporated or grafted into this living organism, thereby sacramentally dying and rising with Christ that he might be set free from sin and enter the sphere of the new creation. So, in the words of Basil:

There are two ends proposed in Baptism: on the one hand, the destruction of the body of sin, that it may no longer bear fruit unto death; on the other, that it may live to the Spirit and have its fruit in sanctification. Now the water expresses the likeness of death, for it receives, as it were, the body into a tomb, but the Spirit is the source of the quickening power, by renewing our souls and bringing them from the deadness of sin into the life that was originally theirs.

Finally, when the Church is the Bride of Christ, baptism is the instrument of adoption and rebirth. So according to Cyprian: 'The second birth, which is in Baptism, begets children of God. Now if the Bride of Christ is one, and she is the Catholic Church, it is the Church herself who begets children for God' and thereby becomes their mother.

Baptism, because it involves incorporation into the Church, is primarily concerned with the individual and is unrepeatable; the Eucharist, on the other hand, is concerned with the community as a whole and is regularly celebrated. Its origins lie in the Last Supper when, according to the earliest written account of it by Paul in his First Epistle to the Corinthians: 'The Lord Jesus in the night in which he was betrayed took bread; and when he had given thanks, he brake it, and said, This is my body, which is for you: this do in remembrance of me. In like manner also the cup, after supper, saying, This cup is the new covenant in my blood: this do, as oft as ye drink it, in remembrance of me.'

In the early part of the Apostolic Age the Eucharist consisted of a repetition of the whole of the Last Supper, meal included, together with other elements of a more free character, traces of which are to be found in the New Testament references to prophecy, speaking with tongues and their interpretation. Side by side with these manifestations of the free activity of the Spirit, there were also features which tended to assume a fixed liturgical form. These comprised instruction, preaching, the Lord's Prayer, the kiss of peace, psalms, hymns, and doxologies, the reading of such apostolic writings as were to hand and possibly of passages from the Old Testament. The removal of the meal proper, to which allusion has already been made when speaking of the agape, opened the way to considerable development which differed in different areas although the basic structure remained everywhere recognizably the same.

According to this fundamental pattern the rite was divided into two parts. The first of these came to be known as the Synaxis, a Greek word meaning 'gathering' or 'assembling' to-gether, or the Mass of the Catechumens, i.e. that part of the service which the candidates for baptism were allowed to attend and at the end of which they were dismissed. The second part was the Eucharist, a Greek word meaning 'thanksgiving' which emphasizes that worship is man's thankful response to the divine act, or the Mass of the Faithful.

The Synaxis in the second century is described for us very simply by Justin: 'On the day which is called Sunday, there is an assembly in the same place of all who live in cities or country districts; and the records of the Apostles, or the writings of the Prophets, are read as long as we have time. Then the reader concludes, and the president verbally instructs and exhorts us to the imitation of these excellent things.' This could equally well be an account of what took place in a Jewish synagogue, and indeed the Synaxis was in the main a reproduc-tion of this with the addition of certain Christian writings to the reading list, so that there were sometimes three, sometimes as many as five lections. The basic pattern which emerges from a comparative study of contemporary documents was then as follows: 1. Opening Greeting. 2. Lesson. 3. Psalm. 4. Lesson (or Lessons separated by Psalms). 5. Sermon. 6. Dismissal of those not belonging to the Church. 7. Prayers. It will be noted that it was not until the final item that prayer was offered, after the withdrawal of the catechumens, and the reason for this lay in the Christian understanding of prayer, that it is made through the Spirit, so that those who had not been made partakers of the Spirit through baptism were unable to participate. When Church worship became more 'public' in the fourth century, when the majority of those present were nominally Christian, and as the institution of the catechumenate progressively declined, alterations began to be made in the Synaxis to provide it with more elements of vocal praise and prayer and with a less abrupt opening. These alterations were largely in the form of additions made at different times in different places by local churches, more isolated with the break-up of the empire, acting with a certain degree of independence. The result was that elaborate and distinct forms appeared which partly obscured the basic outline. An entrance chant was widely adopted; the note of praise was sounded in the East by the Trisagion—'Holy God, Holy Mighty, Holy Immortal, have mercy upon us', repeated three times—and in the West by the *Gloria in Excelsis*, and prayers, diverse in their form and content, monologues by the celebrant or litanies conducted by a deacon, were inserted at different points. The recital of the 'Nicene' Creed was accepted in parts of the East from the fifth century onwards, but only gradually spread through the West to reach Rome in the eleventh century. So what had been primitively a Ministry of the Word, centring in instruction, assumed the character of a devotional preparation for what was to follow.

The structure of the second part of the rite depended directly upon the actions of Jesus at the Last Supper, when he (1) took bread, (2) blessed it, (3) broke it, (4) distributed it. Then came the meal, after which he (5) took the cup, (6) blessed it and (7) distributed it. The removal of the meal from the centre of this brought the several actions closer together so that the Mass of the Faithful came to consist of: (1) Bringing of bread and wine, (2) taking them together, (3) blessing them, (4) breaking the bread and (5) distributing them.

We may see this essential shape quite clearly in Hippolytus by bringing together the two accounts he has preserved.

1. *Bringing or Offertory.*
Then let the oblation at once be brought by the deacons to the bishop.

2. *Taking.*
And he, with all the presbyters, laying his hand on the oblation, shall say, giving thanks:

3. *Blessing or Consecration Prayer.*
The Lord be with you. And the people shall say: And with thy spirit. Lift up your hearts. We have them with the Lord. Let us give thanks unto the Lord. It is meet and right. And forthwith he shall continue thus: We render thanks unto thee, O God, through thy beloved child Jesus Christ, whom in the last times thou didst send to us to be a Saviour and Redeemer and the Messenger of thy counsel; who is thy Word inseparable, through whom thou madest all things and in whom thou wast well pleased; whom thou didst send from heaven into the Virgin's womb and who conceived within her was made flesh and demonstrated to be thy Son being born of the Holy Spirit and a Virgin; who fulfilling thy will and preparing for thee a holy people, stretched forth his hands for suffering that he might release from suffering those who have believed in thee; who when he was betrayed to voluntary suffering that he might abolish death and rend the bond of the devil and tread down hell and enlighten the righteous and establish the ordinance and demonstrate the resurrection: taking bread and giving thanks to thee said: Take eat: this is my body which is broken for you. Likewise also the cup, saying: This is my blood which is shed for you. When you do this, you perform my recalling. Performing therefore the recalling of his death and resurrection, we offer to thee the bread and the cup giving thanks to thee because thou hast bidden us to stand before thee and minister as priests to thee. And we pray that thou wouldest grant to all thy saints who partake to be united to thee that they may be fulfilled with the

Holy Spirit for the confirmation of their faith in truth, that we may praise and glorify thee through thy beloved Child Jesus Christ through whom glory and honour be unto thee with the Holy Spirit in thy holy Church now and for ever and world without end. Amen.

4. *Breaking of Bread or Fraction.*
And when the bishop breaks the bread:

5. *Distribution.*
In distributing to each a fragment, he shall say: The bread of heaven in Christ Jesus. And he who receives shall answer: Amen. And the presbyters—but if there are not enough, the deacons also—shall hold the cups and stand by in good order and with reverence. And they who partake shall taste of it thrice, he who gives saying: In God the Father Almighty; and he who receives shall say: Amen. And in the Lord Jesus Christ; and in the Holy Spirit in the holy Church; and he shall say: Amen. So shall it be done to each one.

In this early third-century account the essential shape of the Eucharist is still clearly discernible, but the words accompanying and commenting on the actions were not, even at this period, regarded as sacrosanct, and so Hippolytus, recognizing that the celebrant was at liberty to use prayers of his own devising, stated that he was only providing a model. Where such freedom was acknowledged, great diversity was to be expected, and when more stereotyped formulae became the norm differences were bound to exist because of the local and even individual prototypes which had preceded them. Hence the rite at Jerusalem would inevitably differ from that at Constantinople and both from that at Rome—local uses were in fact the order of the day and there are extant, from the fourth and fifth centuries, a great number of liturgies which, apart from agreement on the basic structure, have their own peculiarities and distinguishing features. Three principal factors contributed to this result; first, the theological approach of those who helped to bring them to their classical shape; second, local ways of performing the actions which were not the same in all areas, and third, the tendency towards elaboration which has already been noted in connection with the Synaxis. It thus becomes necessary, as a preliminary to a consideration of the further development, to examine the meaning of the rite, and for convenience of exposition to adopt the same method as for baptism, i.e. the definition of the various aspects of eucharistic theology in connexion with the several images of the Church.

If the Church is the Messianic Community, then the Eucharist is the foretaste of the Messianic Banquet, i.e. of the feast which was expected to be provided by the Messiah for his people in the Age to Come. It is the occasion too of the renewal of the new covenant which had been sealed by the blood of Christ upon the cross. If the Church is the Temple of the Divine Presence, then the Eucharist is the sacrifice of the priestly community, and it may be said to be a sacrifice in three ways. It is a sacrifice in that it consists of the offering of bread and wine to God. It is a sacrifice in that under the form of these oblations the Church offers herself to God in union with the heavenly offering of the eternal High Priest. It is a sacrifice in that it recalls, i.e. makes present by its effects, the sacrifice of Christ. If the Church is the Body of Christ, then the Eucharist is the means whereby the Church becomes what it is; by feeding on the sacramental Body of Christ it becomes more truly itself. Further the Eucharist is the means of perpetuating and renewing the unity between the Body and its Head and between the members. Finally, if the Church is the Bride of Christ, then it is through the Eucharist that spiritual sustenance is provided for those children whose mother the Church has become through baptism.

The extent to which emphasis is laid upon any one of these

facets of eucharistic theology will obviously involve differences between separate rites, but the principal differentiating factor is to be found in a further theological theme which concerns the nature of consecration. Consecration means the setting apart of something as sacred to God, the solemn dedication of something to a religious purpose, the making of something holy. It is indeed the technical term for the third of the actions defined above, viz. the blessing of the elements of bread and wine, and it involves the sacramental principle enunciated at the beginning of this chapter, i.e. that of taking the particular in order to represent the relation of the whole to God. So a specific quantity of bread and wine is consecrated or set apart by blessing it that it may be the means of communion with the risen and ascended Christ.

In the early days of the Church this blessing, following Jewish practice, was believed to be effected by thanking God for certain acts. So in the 'consecration' prayer of Hippolytus, quoted above, God is thanked for creation and redemption through Christ. In course of time however a new conception of blessing entered Christian thought with the idea that God's Name was put upon the food which was thereby changed and became charged with divine power. This had diverse effects in East and West. In the West consecration became identified with the recitation of the Words of Institution, i.e. of the narrative of the Last Supper, while in the East it was identified with an invocation of God to send down the Holy Spirit upon the elements—this latter invocation was known as the Epiclesis. It is at this point that notice must be taken of a difference in the way of doing things which, in conjunction with these two understandings of consecration, led to a considerable change in the internal structure of the Eucharist. The Offertory or bringing up of the bread and wine took place in the West immediately before the prayer of consecration when the worshippers each brought his or her offering of bread and wine to be received by the deacons who gave them to the celebrant. In the East these gifts were accepted before the service began and were prepared in a side chapel. This preparation was soon elaborated into what is known as the rite of the Prothesis when Christ was symbolically slain by the piercing of the bread with a miniature lance. At the Offertory the dead Christ was then borne in a solemn procession, known as the Great Entrance, and this was connected with the Epiclesis by the belief that at the invocation the dead Christ was raised by the Spirit and so became present as the living Lord in the midst of the faithful. In this way the primitive structure was elaborated and overlaid and Eastern and Western rites diverged in form.

Local uses persisted for many centuries, so that in the West there were such rites as the Ambrosian at Milan, the Gallican in France and the Mozarabic in Spain, while in the East there were the Armenian, the Coptic and the Syrian. Gradually, in both areas, one of these tended to assume a position of pre-dominance—the Roman rite in the West and the Byzantine or Constantinopolitan in the East—thus leading to a greater measure of uniformity. This uniformity was accompanied by two growing emphases, the first on the awesomeness and wonder of the service and the second on the function of the celebrant who became more and more a lone authoritative figure doing something in the presence of a passive congregation rather than the leader of a corporate action in which each had a part to play, and so issuing in the non-communicating attendance and private masses of the Middle Ages.

At this point it is necessary to interrupt this description of the development of Christian worship in its broad outlines in order to say something of the buildings in which it was con-ducted. The inner life of the Church, experienced through its sacraments, assumes more life and meaning when it is studied in close association with its architectural setting apart from which it is something of an abstraction. Christian worship was at first primarily a domestic affair, centring in a meal and taking place in a private house, and for many centuries no special buildings were erected. In recent years archaeological research has brought to light quite a number of these house-churches, four at Rome from the third and fourth centuries, one in England at Lullingstone in Kent dating from c. A.D. 345 and a sixth, the earliest of all, at Dura Europos on the Euphrates dating from A.D. 230. An impending attack of the Persians upon this outpost of the empire led to the construction of a vast earthwork under which the house-church was completely buried and thereby preserved. Access from the street was obtained by a single entrance door in the north wall which opened into a vestibule and thence into a court. On the east side of this court there was a portico and along the other three sides five rooms were disposed. In the north-west corner was the baptistery, richly decorated with frescoes, its font surmounted by a canopy. Opposite to this, along the southern wall of the house, two rooms had been made into one, at the east end of which there was a small platform for the altar and a door to the side led into the sacristy. The use of the other room along the west wall is doubtful, but drawings on the walls suggest that it was employed as a classroom for catechumens.

Even this simple arrangement represents a development, for at first the Eucharist was celebrated in the dining-room around a table, whereas at Dura a special platform has been provided for the altar, while baptism, as we have seen, took place in rivers and lakes, whereas at Dura a font has been introduced. Further development became essential with the increase in the size of congregations which could no longer be accommodated in a private dwelling. The church however remained a house with its main room greatly enlarged, i.e. the complex of buildings included not only a hall for worship, but also rooms where the clergy could live, eat and sleep, a hostelry where travellers could find shelter for the night, an almonry where the deacons could distribute charity to the poor, a baptistery, and, in some towns, even baths to allow Christians toilet facilities free from the temptations encountered in the public baths.

The form adopted for the principal enlarged room is known as the basilica and there is every reason to suppose that it was copied by the Christians from those pagan buildings, which already bore the same name, used as courts of law and as exchanges. The basilica, as modified by Christian usage, was a rectangular hall with its entrance in one of the shorter sides opposite a semicircular apse in the other. In the centre of this apse, which was raised a little above the level of the main floor and was roofed by a half dome, the bishop had his *cathedra* or seat, on either side of which were benches for the presbyters. In front of the episcopal throne, often on the chord of the apse, was the altar around which the deacons were grouped. This frequently stood above a *confessio* or repository for the relics of a saint and beneath a *ciborium* or canopy. The body of the church was divided by parallel rows of columns into aisles of which there was usually an uneven number. The centre one, the nave, corresponded to the apse in width, and its upper walls, supported by the columns, rose above the lean-to roofs of the side-aisles and allowed daylight direct admission through a row of windows. The congregation was expected to stand, except for the aged and infirm for whom wooden or stone benches were at times provided. Men and women were carefully separated, but the method of separation differed from region to region. In Greek lands galleries were provided over the side aisles for the women, but where these were absent the disposition could be either transverse, the men being across the naves and aisles at the front and behind them the women, or longitudinal, in which case the men were generally on the right and the women on the left. The final division of the hall was the porch in which catechumens and penitents were allowed to stand, but in the Greek basilica this vestibule was incorporated into the main structure being known as the *narthex*.

The basilica, in one form or another, had an area of distribution ranging from Mesopotamia and Syria to Great Britain. In the West it was perpetuated for over a thousand years, but in the East it ceased to be in general use after the fifth century when it was ousted by churches of the central type, i.e. buildings which are not rectangular but round, octagonal or square and surmounted usually by a dome.

The chief factor operating to produce this typically Eastern form of church architecture was the cult of the saints. In the West, where relics were placed in close proximity to the altar, this cult developed in association with the Eucharist within the one building. In the East however these relics were at first preserved in separate buildings which assumed the traditional form of tombs, round, octagonal, square, etc. In the latter half of the fifth century the practice of translating relics allowed the cult of the martyrs to be brought into the church building itself and with it came the architectural forms which had originally enshrined them. It was from these memorial edifices that the churches of the central type evolved, becoming henceforth predominant in the eastern Mediterranean.

The baptistery too, because of the connexion between the rite and the burial of Christ, tended to assume the same form— although the influence of the public baths must also be noted —round, square and octagonal buildings were common. The fonts were habitually sunk beneath the level of the floor and the steps leading down into them were taken to symbolize the union of the believer with Christ in his death. Since the candidates had to disrobe, a dressing-room was a necessity. More important was the provision of a place where the ceremony could be completed, since it was for centuries the practice of the Church to baptize and confirm at the same time;

baptism and confirmation forming one united rite of Christian initiation. The chamber used for this was known as the *consignatorium*, placed close to the *pistikon* where the catechumens had recited the creed.

Since it was the office of the bishop to confirm and since baptism and confirmation were for long united, baptisteries were at first built only in the episcopal cities, although a few other towns possessed them in order to spare the candidates too long a journey. Until the two halves of the rite were finally separated this scarcity of baptisteries continued and it was not until the eleventh century in the West that every parish had its own. In the East, where from an early date the priest was allowed to confirm with oil which had been episcopally blessed, baptisteries were much more numerous and were by no means confined to episcopal centres. In parts of Syria by the sixth century every town had its baptistery, not infrequently two and sometimes apparently three.

For a full appreciation of these buildings a knowledge of their plans and interior arrangements is not in itself sufficient, since, as a setting for worship, they were lavishly decorated. This embellishment included not only sculptured ornament, such as the finely modelled capitals and the delicate tracery of the balustrades, the chiselled doors and the elaborate canopies that frequently stood over the altar, the patterned episcopal thrones and the carved pulpits used at first for the reading of the Scriptures, it included also the walls which were richly adorned with either frescoes or mosaics.

Although the early Christians adopted the styles and the techniques familiar in the pagan world, they were the first to make use of mosaic as a mural decoration on a large scale and to realize the full splendour of the colour effects it can produce. By embedding tesserae or small cubes of coloured glass, each at a slightly different angle, in a foundation of cement, they were able to reflect the light in a manner at once luminous and resplendent. No one who has seen the magnificent mosaics in St. Maria Maggiore at Rome (432–40), in St. Vitale at Ravenna (521–34) or in the almost contemporary St. Apollinare in Classe can fail to admire this offering to God of man's supreme creative ability. These ambitious schemes of decoration were intended not only to beautify the Church's worship but also to instruct the worshipper—they were in fact the illiterate man's Bible and their subject matter was largely drawn from the Scriptures. Scenes from the life of Christ were therefore common and the Old Testament was laid under contribution for a whole series of events which were taken to foreshadow or typify the Gospel story. If the step from the Upper Room in Jerusalem to the glories of Sancta Sophia at Constantinople (563) seems a long one, it may be regarded as but the natural working out of man's thankful response to the divine initiative, a response which is emphasized by the name of the principal Christian act of worship, i.e. the Eucharist or Thanksgiving.

Simply and solely because it was the main service, the Eucharist was associated with two other aspects of Christian life, viz. marriage and burial. Christian marriage customs owed not a little to pagan practices which the Church was quite willing to accept. As soon as an agreement had been reached between a man and a woman as to their intention to be united in wedlock, they imparted the news to an officer of the Church and a day of betrothal was fixed. Then the parties assembled at the house of the bride's father, in the presence of as many as ten witnesses, the bride being dressed in white. The man made his offering of money which was at the same time both a pledge of his sincerity and an assurance that the woman would thereafter share his worldly goods. A ring was then placed upon the third finger of the woman's left hand, and the betrothal was completed by a solemn kiss and the joining of hands. On the wedding day the couple proceeded to church, accompanied by their friends; during the first two or three centuries the bride was arrayed in a veil which she had worn since her betrothal; later she received it from the hands of the priest as part of the marriage ceremonial. The service itself began with prayers on behalf of the couple who next declared their free consent to the contract between them; the officiating minister joined their hands and pronounced a blessing upon their union. Next in the East, or at the conclusion of the entire service in the West, crowns were placed on their heads and the Eucharist was celebrated. 'How,' asked Tertullian, 'shall we describe the happiness of a marriage which is cemented by the Church, ratified by the oblation and sealed with the benediction?' An agape in the house of the bride's father followed, after which a joyful procession accompanied the newly wedded pair to their home; the husband carried his bride over the threshold, gave her a bunch of keys as a token of her authority over the household, while she untied her hair as a symbol of his authority over her.

If Christian marriage had many features in common with pagan rites, Christian burial was remarkable for its contrasts as befitted a religion which laid such emphasis upon the doctrine of the resurrection. At the death-bed the words of the *ordo commendationis animae* were recited by a priest:

> Deliver, O Lord, his soul, as thou hast delivered:
>> Enoch and Elijah from the common death,
>> Noah from the flood,
>> Abraham from the city of Ur of the Chaldees,
>> Job from his sufferings,
>> Isaac from sacrifice and from the hand of his father Abraham,
>> Lot from Sodom and from the fire,
>> Moses from the hand of Pharaoh, king of Egypt,
>> Daniel from the lions' den,
>> The three children from the fiery furnace and the hand of the perverse king,

Susannah from false accusations,
David from the hand of Saul and from the hand of Goliath,
Peter and Paul from prison.

And also as thou hast delivered the blessed Thecla, thy virgin and martyr, from fearful torments, so also stoop to receive the soul of thy servant and grant it to rejoice with thee in the heavenly riches.

As soon as death had taken place the eyes of the deceased were closed, his body was washed and anointed and then wrapped in a white linen cloth. On the day of the funeral the corpse was carried upon a bier, accompanied by his friends, all wearing white, not pagan black, and bearing not funeral cypresses but palms and olive branches as the symbols of victory over death. Others carried thuribles smoking with incense and lighted lamps to the accompaniment of hymns of hope and joy. When they reached the grave, further prayers were offered and an address was delivered by the bishop or a presbyter. Then the Eucharist was celebrated in token of the communion that still existed between the living and the dead. The corpse was saluted with a last kiss of peace and the tomb was sealed. An agape normally followed, terminating upon a note of quiet joy—there were no hired mourners—in the belief that the deceased had entered upon his rest in the company of his Master.

It was not only these solemn occasions in human life that the Church sought to sanctify—birth through baptism, marriage and death—but the whole of human existence through the regular celebration of the Eucharist and time itself was to be sanctified by the observance of the Church's calendar. In the ante-Nicene period three principal festivals were observed, viz. Easter Day and Pentecost, and Sunday as the weekly memorial of the resurrection of Christ. But these were not commemorations of historical events, rather they were 'feasts of ideas' representing the inauguration of the Age to Come, i.e. they were eschatological in significance. Christians of this period in fact took little interest in time as such, for they were confident that they were living 'in the last times', that 'the fashion of this world passeth away', and so, in the words of Cyprian, 'he who hopes for eternity from God does not celebrate the seasons of earth any more'. In the fourth century the need to hallow the daily life of the multitude of nominal Christians encouraged a rapid development of the calendar by the inclusion in it of more and more specifically historical commemorations. A lead was given to this movement by the church of Jerusalem, for it was natural that the regular celebration of the events in the life of Christ should receive an impetus from the place so intimately connected with the events themselves. So by the last quarter of the fourth century Passion Sunday, Palm Sunday, Maundy Thursday, Good Friday and Easter Day were all being observed with great dignity and dramatic display—processions, vigils and the Eucharist all helping to bring home to the laity the truths of the Gospel. To this cycle of events Lent was soon added. As early as the second century it had been the custom to set aside some weeks before Easter for the instruction of the catechumens and by the end of the fourth century this had been extended in many areas to the familiar forty days and associated with Christ's fast in the wilderness.

At the same time, the observance of Christmas was spreading throughout the Church. The choice of December 25th was no doubt due to the pagan connexions of the day, for it was originally a great heathen winter festival and the Church sought to direct the people's habits into Christian channels. In the East, January 6th was at first kept as Christ's birthday, but in the late fourth century there was an interchange, and January 6th was adopted as the Epiphany, the time of the showing of Jesus to the Gentiles in the persons of the three wise men. Once the birthday and the day of Christ's death had been fixed other commemorations followed in due course; thus the Circumcision was eight days after Christmas and the Annunciation nine months before; the Ascension was forty days after Easter, Whitsunday ten days after that, and so on. So the calendar was gradually elaborated; Advent for example, as a period of preparation for Christmas, being adopted in Gaul in the sixth century.

Concurrently with this development of the cycle of Christ's life, there also emerged a calendar of saints. In the first days of the Church the term 'saint' was applied to all its members, but in time the indisputable fact that many Christians were far from perfect led to the limitation of this title to those men and women, in particular the martyrs, whose discipleship approximated to the ideal. Already by the middle of the second century, Christians had begun to commemorate the days on which martyrs had been executed, celebrating the Eucharist upon or close to their tombs. The practice spread rapidly and was encouraged by Church leaders who saw in it a means of imbuing local patriotism with the Christian spirit by replacing the ancient pagan heroes and local deities by those local saints and martyrs whose example had been an inspiration to many. Hence at first calendars were primarily local, and although eventually additions were made, being borrowed from other churches, a practice encouraged by the translation of relics, this roll of honour never lost this original characteristic. The Church's calendar in its more or less final and stereotyped form was the result of the fusion of these two separate cycles, viz. the events in the life of Christ and the days consecrated to the saints. Of this scheme the regular celebration of the Eucharist was the centre, but services of a non-sacramental character were also held, and these were known as the Offices.

In his life of Chrysostom, Palladius records how the

bishop arranged an evening service of psalms and inter-
cessions for the male members of his congregation whose work
had prevented any devotions during the day. This was but one
of the many factors that led to the establishing of a regular
round of weekday assemblies for worship. Already at the
opening of the third century Hippolytus had recommended
seven hours of prayer; he had, that is to say, systematized daily
private prayer, and the step was but a short one from obliga-
tory prayer at home to common prayer in church, just as it
needed little to change directions as to prayer into directions
as to what prayers to say. The monastic movement, with its
pattern of frequent acts of worship, gave a great impetus to
this and by the end of the fourth century the development was
complete, the hours having each their appointed psalms with
provision for systematic Bible reading.

'Strangers and pilgrims'—that was how the early Christians thought of themselves, and regarded it as their duty to keep
themselves 'unspotted from the world'. To the realization of
this ideal the forces of paganism and secularism proved a constant menace, and it was only by the maintenance of its inner
life of prayer and worship that the Church was able to pursue
its mission without that entire capitulation and corruption that
would have marked its failure. That a knowledge of the supernatural and a hope of salvation were kept alive throughout
what is commonly called the Dark Ages was dependent upon
the Church's spiritual health based upon its allegiance to its
Lord and the presence of the Holy Spirit.

8

The Beliefs of the Church

THE Church was not only a worshipping community, wit-
nessing by its life to the reality of the divine action whereby it had been called into being, it was also a believing community. The formulation of these beliefs was a slow process,
for this growth towards self-consciousness required the seeking of answers to questions that were so complex that solution
after solution had to be discarded before there was general
agreement that all the essential factors had been related and
none had been omitted. These beliefs as ultimately defined
were an interpretation of Christian experience not only as set
down in the apostolic writings but as a continuing element,
even basis, of everyday life in the community amidst the
strains and stresses of the world. The doctrines thus enunciated
were not intended to be substitutes for that experience but a
map or guide to it in order to ensure clear and accurate thinking about God and the rejection of wrong or fallacious ideas
which would inevitably undermine the truth and therefore the
effectiveness of the Gospel.

In this quest for the clarification of belief certain fixed
elements interacted with others that were more flexible.
Amongst the former must be listed the Bible, in its complete
form, for even before the closure of the canon the authority of
the apostolic writings was generally recognized. To this must

be added the *lex orandi* or rule of prayer and worship and the *regula fidei* or rule of faith, for if the forms of worship became more elaborate and the quasi-creedal formulae more stylized, their content remained much the same. As for the flexible elements, these included the change from the Hebrew technique of pictorial thinking to the more precise thought-forms of Greek metaphysics, the invention and acceptance of an exact terminology and the differences in temperament, capability and approach of the individual theologians who gave themselves to the task of elucidation.

Those to whom the Church proclaimed its Gospel were in no need of being persuaded of the existence of spiritual reality; they were fully aware of it. They knew too their own inner disunity and appreciated that this was the outcome of their being disunited from the divine realm. They sought therefore a means to bridge the gulf and secure peace and communion with the divine. In Christ, so the Church affirmed, at-one-ment with God was now possible; man's condition of sin or rebellion against God had been radically altered by the advent of the Saviour; the 'Way' was now open to live a life in total reliance upon and communion with God. The understanding of this experience of salvation differed from centre to centre and from century to century—indeed the Church to this day has not laid down any particular interpretation as sufficiently comprehensive to enshrine the whole truth.

To the second-century Apologists, anxious to commend the faith to the educated pagan, Christianity was the true philosophy. Christ is the Revelation of God and salvation is enlightenment. 'Through Jesus Christ,' according to I Clement, 'God has called us from darkness to light, from ignorance to the knowledge of his glorious Name.' Christ thus brings the perfect knowledge of God and liberates man from ignorance and error. But salvation was also considered to involve liberation in another sense, i.e. the setting free of man from sin and death and from the power of evil spirits. Christ is the triumphant Conqueror who has overthrown Satan and his minions in a decisive battle that ensured final victory, although skirmishes still continue. Two explanations as to how this conquest had been effected were forthcoming. On the one hand it was said that the devil, in attacking Jesus, mistakenly believing him to be only a man, was overthrown by the Godhead whom he was unable to hold captive, and on the other that the devil, having acquired certain rights over man on account of his sin, was paid off by the sufferings and death of Christ and could have no further claims over mankind. This mythology of man's deliverance from Satan was however by no means as cogent as the theory of recapitulation largely developed by Irenaeus.

Recapitulation can mean either 'going over the ground again' or 'restoration into unity'. In the former sense Christ is the Second Adam who went over the same ground as the first but with the opposite result; where Adam yielded to temptation, Christ overcame. So sharing all the experiences of man from birth to death, sin only excepted, he rose triumphant over death and, as Adam was the originator of a rebellious race doomed to destruction, so he became the fountain head of a new, redeemed humanity assured of eternal life. In the latter sense God and man, divided by sin, are made one in Christ who embodied in himself the whole of human history as purposed by God in his original creation. Consequently to experience salvation is to enter upon a life of unity with God through Christ and in him with one's fellow men.

Also to be found in the teaching of Irenaeus, although receiving much less emphasis than his theory of recapitulation, is the thesis that salvation is divinization: Christ 'out of his great love became what we are that he might make us what he is himself'. This indeed became one of the main features of the Alexandrian explanation of the meaning of salvation, and it is necessary to recognize that, as the Church grew, different emphases came to be found in different parts of the empire.

In the West, where the sense of law and order was strong, Christians tended to place their emphasis upon the practical rather than the speculative and to interpret salvation primarily in legal terms. Sin, to them, was a crime against God requiring satisfaction. But since man was unable to render satisfaction and was consequently under condemnation, God himself intervened to vindicate his law and pay the debt. So, according to Jerome, Christ 'endured in our stead the penalty we ought to have suffered for our crimes'. He offered himself as a sacrifice on man's behalf, hence, in the words of Augustine, 'we were brought to death by sin, he by righteousness, and so, since death was our penalty for sin, his death became a sacrifice for sin'. To the Westerns the main stress is therefore to be laid on Calvary, on the meritorious death when the life blood was freely given as the price of reconciliation, and salvation means the forgiveness of sins mediated through the vicarious and sacrificial death of Christ.

In the East there were two main theological schools, the one centring in Antioch and the other in Alexandria, each having its own principal line of approach. The Antiochenes considered man to be in a state of corruption because of his disobedience to the divine will. To restore the true relationship of God and man the divine intervention was necessary involving the creation of a new Man who would live in perfect obedience to God. At the Incarnation the Son of God united man to himself and, consummating a life-long obedience by the death on the cross, triumphed over corruption through his resurrection.

If the West emphasized the Crucifixion and the school of Antioch the Resurrection, the Alexandrians concentrated upon the Incarnation, holding to the theory of divinization that had previously found expression in Irenaeus among others. To them the primary consequence of sin was man's corruption, the defacing of the divine image and the loss of immortality. He required therefore restoration and it was to this end that the Divine Image in the person of Christ united man to himself. In his *De Incarnatione* Athanasius gave this belief very clear expression: 'None other could restore a corruptible being to incorruption but the Saviour who in the beginning made everything out of nothing. None other could re-create man according to the image, but he who is the Father's Image. None other could make a mortal being immortal, but he who is Life itself, our Lord Jesus Christ.' Thus Christ came into the world to effect man's deification: 'He became man that we might become divine.' By the unification of the manhood and the Godhead in him, human corruptibility was overcome and man was made superior to death, entering upon a process of deification whereby he could attain his true end, not by being transformed into the Godhead but by receiving immortality and the final blessing of the divine vision.

It was upon this intricate basis of the Christian experience of salvation that Christian doctrine in all its ramifications was erected, for this experience prompted a number of questions, e.g. what exactly is the relationship between Jesus the Saviour and the Supreme God who had sent him? How, granted that salvation is a reality, is the person of Jesus to be understood? The first of these led to the formulation of the doctrine of the Trinity and the second to the investigation of what is known as the Christological problem.

In seeking to trace the development of the doctrine of the Trinity a convenient starting point is the experience of an individual believer typical of all others. The apostle Thomas, or doubting Thomas as he is more familiarly known, had been brought up in the faith that there is one God, the Creator of heaven and earth. When he became a follower of Jesus, there was no reason for him to give up this belief but eventually, after the Resurrection, he was compelled to recognize his master as 'My Lord and my God', and finally to acknowledge the divine power energizing within him, the Holy Spirit, as in some sense also God. Thus while adhering firmly to the monotheism which was part of his Jewish inheritance, he was driven by his experience to express belief in God the Father, God the Son and God the Holy Spirit. His problem and that of the early Church as a whole was how to reconcile these two articles of faith, viz. the oneness of God and the divine triplicity.

The apostolic writers sought to resolve this problem by pressing into service the Jewish idea of intermediaries between God and the world. So Paul saw in Jesus the Wisdom of God, and, following the book of Proverbs, ascribed to him in this capacity pre-existence and agency in the act of creation; Jesus was therefore the Image of God and 'in him dwelleth all the fulness of the Godhead bodily'. The author of the Epistle to the Hebrews, also using Wisdom phraseology, describes him as 'the effulgence of the divine glory, and the very image of his substance'. In the preface to the Fourth Gospel Jesus is identified with the Word of God, i.e. the final revelation of the creative thought and purpose of God, and he is declared to be the unique Son of the Father with whom he enjoys the most intimate communion. These same Old Testament categories were used in the second century and so according to Justin Martyr: 'God begat in the beginning before all creatures a certain rational power from himself, who is called by the Holy Spirit, now the Glory of the Lord, now the Son, again Wisdom, again an Angel, and then Lord and Word. . . . For he can be called by all those names since he ministers to the Father's will, and since he was begotten of the Father by an act of will.'

In similar biblical vein, Irenaeus, in opposition to the Gnostic reduction of the Son and the Spirit to mere emanations, refers to them as 'the two Hands of God' in order to bring out the indissoluble unity between the creative Father and the organs of his activity. But in the second century it was the idea of Christ as the Word that was to the fore. Thinking of God, not like later theologians as three co-equal persons but as one person possessing a mind and his wisdom, they regarded Christ as the Word, i.e. the divine reason or thought of God which received a relative independence or distinction when it was expressed. They were thus able to safeguard the oneness of the Godhead while at the same time asserting that there are real distinctions in his innermost being. But this position had two weaknesses: on the one hand it depersonalized the Son and the Spirit and on the other it tended to subordinate the Son unduly to the Father and to issue, because of the two meanings of Word, viz. thought and its expression, in the belief that there were two stages in the Word's existence. From eternity he was regarded as indwelling the Father, as reason inhabits the mind; in the act of creation, of which he was the agent, he issued forth as thought does when it is expressed in speech. This in effect was to reduce the Son to an impersonal function of the Father.

Side by side with speculations concerning the Word, other writers were advancing their tentative conclusions, and two such movements of thought found expression at the turn of the century, viz. Adoptionism and Modalism. The originator of the first was a certain leather-worker named Theodotus, who came to Rome c. 190. An ardent rationalist, he asserted that Jesus was no more than a man who was adopted as God's Son at his baptism when the divine power, called Christ or Spirit, descended upon him; this however did not make him divine —although certain of his followers affirmed his deification after the Resurrection—and so the oneness of God was unimpaired. The principal leader of the second was a cleric from the Pentapolis named Sabellius who reached Rome c. 215. He taught that the Godhead is a monad expressing itself in three modes or operations; so Father, Son and Holy Spirit are but designations for one and the same being manifesting itself in different modes; the teaching is thus essentially unitarianism. Neither of these lines of thought ultimately commended itself to the Church at large, the one because it denied the divinity of Jesus, apart from which salvation could not be a reality, and the other because it made nonsense of the intimate communion of Father and Son which is so noticeable a feature of the Gospel record and suggested that God had been responsible for an unnecessary fiction in revealing himself under different names which corresponded to no eternal realities. These were not so much solutions of the problem of multiplicity in unity as evasions of it. Contemporary theologians, in combating these errors, took further steps forward in the process of elucidation and their thinking was not a little influenced by philosophical discussions of the nature of unity.

The terminology centres in the words genus, species and individual. A genus is a class of things or beings of the same type, having certain attributes in common. A species is a sub-division of a genus and is also a class of beings or things of the same type with common characteristics. An individual, according to the Aristotelian definition, is that which is one in number and the difference between individuals is a difference in number. So a man and a dog belong to the same genus, viz. the animal—they are one according to unity of genus. Peter and Paul belong to the same species, viz. the human—they are one according to unity of species. But Peter and Paul are also individuals and they are therefore two. A further type of unity to be noted is unity of substratum; thus two pennies are one because their substratum or underlying substance is one, viz. copper. Turning now to Tertullian and approaching the Godhead from the aspect of its plurality, he is emphatic that Father, Son and Holy Spirit are three, not one; they are numerically distinct and capable of being counted, hence they are three individuals. But since there is only one of each of these individuals, one Father, one Son and one Spirit, they are not only individuals but species: each is therefore an individual species and Tertullian can call them persons, meaning thereby individual subsistences. This, it will be noted, is an advance upon his predecessors who tended to think of God as one person with his Word and Spirit immanent within him. From the aspect of its unity, the Godhead is one according to unity of substratum, i.e. Father, Son and Holy Spirit have one underlying substance which has no existence apart from them. This substance is the very being of deity of which the Father is the source, since the Son is begotten by him and the Spirit proceeds from him. This involves no division or separation but is the basis of unity, just as there is unity between the root and its shoot, the source and the river and the sun and its light. 'I always maintain,' says Tertullian, 'one substance in three who cohere.' This is his expression of the 'economy', i.e. the interior organization and constructive integration of the Godhead. It was this formulation, albeit without a full understanding of the organic basis of unity involved in this use of the term 'economy', that was eventually accepted by the Western Church as a correct and intelligible expression of the Christian experience of the Godhead, and in two important particulars it represents an advance upon previous thought. First Tertullian in North Africa, and his Roman contemporary Hippolytus likewise, emphasized the distinction of the persons and, second, they made a valiant attempt to assert the oneness of the divine substance of which the three are expressions.

In the East, also in the early third century, it was Origen, head of the catechetical school of Alexandria, that pioneered Trinitarian thinking. Like Tertullian, he laid stress on the triplicity, criticizing those who held that Father, Son and Holy Spirit are not numerically distinct and affirming that they are not just three individuals, otherwise they would be three Gods, but three individual species, since each is unique and is not a specimen representative of a class. At the same time they are one, being one genus because the three belong to the same class, that of the Godhead, having certain attributes in common, and they are also one species because, being one God, they are not subdivisions of the one genus. Thus Father, Son and Holy Spirit are three individual species insofar as they are to be distinguished from one another, and they are one insofar as they have a common specific genus. Like Tertullian too, Origen declared that the Father was the fountainhead of the divinity, and he further asserted the eternal generation of Son, i.e. since he was begotten by the Father in eternity, which is by definition outside time, there is no beginning or ending to this process and one cannot say 'there was when he was not'— he thus refuted the two-stage theory of the Word's existence found not only in the Apologists but even in Tertullian. Unfortunately Origen did not rest content with this position but pressing into service many Scriptural citations which were not really relevant to his subject and being unable to distinguish between creation and derivation, he taught a form of subordination of the Son to the Father which bore fruit ultimately in the Arian heresy.

Arius, a presbyter of Alexandria, first came into prominence *c.* 323. His teaching was to the effect that since God is one, unique and indivisible, the Son must be a creature, perfect indeed and not to be compared with the rest of creation, but nevertheless, not being self-existent, he is not truly God; to call him so is merely to make use of a courtesy title, and just as a human son is posterior in time to his father, so the divine Son must be of later existence than the divine Father; hence 'once he was not' since 'before he was begotten he was not'. This was to carry Origen's subordinationism to the extreme and to ignore the stress he laid upon eternal generation, while at the same time opening the door to polytheism because the worship of Christ, which Arius did not discontinue, was on his interpretation the worship of a creature. Moreover it called in question the Christian experience of salvation, since if Christ were not himself divine no fellowship with God could have been re-established through him. Arius' opponents were soon active and in an endeavour to restore peace the emperor Constantine summoned the Council of Nicaea in 325.

This, the first of the ecumenical councils, both condemned Arius and produced a statement of faith which was to affirm the full divinity of the Son and preclude the creaturely status ascribed to him by the heretics. It was therefore stated that the Son was 'begotten not made' and that he was 'of one substance with the Father', i.e. what the Father is so is the Son—he is thus completely God. This left the problem of the divine unity unsolved, but this was not the concern of the Nicene bishops.

In the vanguard of the continuing struggle against Arianism was Athanasius, who became bishop of Alexandria in 328. He based his thought firmly on the Christian experience of salvation and upon his own interpretation of that in terms of divinization: 'the Word could never have divinized us if he were merely divine by participation and were not himself the essential Godhead'. Further Athanasius came to realize that the Greek word adopted into the creed of Nicaea and translated above 'of one substance' could also be rendered 'of one content' and that in this sense it had a bearing upon the relationship of Father and Son. He therefore used it to declare that Christ's complete divinity involved an identity of content of the divine persons; they are therefore one because of their identity of substance. Moreover whereas hitherto the main Trinitarian debate had centred in the unity of Father and Son, it being realized that if there were room in the Godhead for two no problem was presented by a third, Athanasius also applied the idea of identity of content to the Spirit, declaring him to be of one substance with the Father and the Son.

Father, Son and Holy Spirit are thus not three beings but substantially identical and so one being.

Athanasius' teaching was carried further and finally crystallized in the teaching of the Cappadocian trio, Basil of Caesarea, his brother Gregory of Nyssa and their friend Gregory of Nazianzus. Strongly influenced by the thought of Origen, they upheld his belief in a specific genus as the basis of the unity, but discarded his subordinationism by transforming it to explain the differences between the three individual species. The Godhead, so they taught, is one because of identity of being, but each objective presentation of that being is to be distinguished by certain individual characteristics which are in fact modes of existence. Hence the Father is ingenerate, the Son begotten and the Spirit proceeding. These modes of existence refer to the relations between the divine persons and so express eternal processes continually operative within the divine being.

The 'Cappadocian Settlement', as it is sometimes called, became the normative expression of Trinitarian belief in the East, being incorporated by John of Damascus († 749) into his *De Fide Orthodoxa*. At the same time John also made use of the work of an anonymous writer, known as Pseudo-Cyril, who in order to safeguard the unity in Trinity and to avoid lapse into tritheism had emphasized the doctrine of the coinherence or mutual indwelling of the three persons, i.e. the three being in one another are co-terminous and co-extensive. So if one begins from a single substance, expressed objectively in three presentations, the being of God is clearly stated and his unity preserved, and if one begins from the triplicity of the objective presentation one is led back, through the affirmation of their co-inherence, to identity of being, and the same confession results.

In the West meantime Tertullian's conception of a unity of substratum, involving identity of substance, continued to be upheld and it is indeed probable that the acceptance of the term 'of one substance' at Nicaea was due not a little to the Western delegates. Their teaching reached its culmination in the thought of Augustine who had two significant contributions to make. Previously, in accepting the union of substratum, it had been customary to regard the Father as the substratum, i.e. the Godhead common to the three persons was identified with the Father since it was from him that both the Son and the Spirit derived their own Godhead. Hence according to Tertullian 'the Father is the entire substance, but the Son is a derivation or portion of the whole'. Augustine however did not identify the Godhead with the Father but with the substratum common to all three, while at the same time declaring that it had no existence apart from the three. Thus the three are one because they are one substance and they are to be distinguished by their mutual relations. Augustine's second contribution lay in the use of analogies drawn from the structure of human nature on the grounds that some faint traces of the Trinity are discernible within it since it was created in the image of God. So, for example, he refers to the mind, its knowledge of itself and its love of itself, or again to the mind as remembering, thinking and loving God—each is a tri-unity. But all analogies are in the final analysis inadequate, for the unity in Trinity is unique, so according to John Damascene 'it is quite impossible to find in creation an image that will illustrate by itself exactly in all details the nature of the holy Trinity'. The task which these Christian thinkers set themselves was not a vain one but nevertheless it was one of the utmost difficulty and they recognized, in the words of Gregory of Nazianzus, that 'it is difficult to conceive God: but to define him is impossible'. Indeed the truth of the divine being can only be expressed satisfactorily in a series of antitheses, whereby an erroneous interpretation of Christian experience is avoided. In the so-called Athanasian Creed, a semi-liturgical document probably of Gallican origin and dating from the end of the fifth century, we find a classical statement of the necessary antitheses which can stand as a convenient summary of this examination of one of the primary aspects of Christian beliefs:

The Catholic Faith is this: that we worship one God in Trinity, and Trinity in Unity;

Neither confounding the persons: nor dividing the substance.

For there is one person of the Father, another of the Son: and another of the Holy Spirit.

But the Godhead of the Father, of the Son, and of the Holy Spirit, is all one: the glory equal, the majesty co-eternal.

Such as the Father is, such is the Son: and such is the Holy Spirit.

The Father uncreated, the Son uncreated: the Holy Spirit uncreated;

The Father infinite, the Son infinite: the Holy Spirit infinite.

The Father eternal, the Son eternal: the Holy Spirit eternal;

And yet there are not three eternals; but one eternal;

As also there are not three uncreated, nor three infinites: but one infinite, and one uncreated.

So likewise the Father is almighty, the Son almighty: and the Holy Spirit almighty;

And yet there are not three almighties: but one almighty.

So the Father is God, the Son God: the Holy Spirit God;

And yet there are not three Gods: but one God.

So the Father is Lord, the Son Lord: the Holy Spirit Lord;

And yet there are not three Lords; but one Lord.

For like as we are compelled by the Christian verity: to confess each person by himself to be both God and Lord;

So are we forbidden by the Catholic Religion: to speak of three Gods or three Lords.

The Father is made of none: nor created, nor begotten.

The Son is of the Father alone: not made, nor created, but begotten.

The Holy Spirit is of the Father and the Son: not made, nor created, nor begotten, but proceeding.

There is therefore one Father, not three Fathers; one Son, not three Sons; one Holy Spirit, not three Holy Spirits.

And in this Trinity there is no before or after: no greater or less;

But all three persons are co-eternal together: and co-equal.

So that in all ways, as is aforesaid: both the Trinity is to be worshipped in Unity, and the Unity in Trinity.

The Trinitarian question was the main concern of Christian thinkers in the first three and a half centuries; only when it was approaching its solution was attention directed to the Christological problem which, while not entirely neglected, had hitherto received nothing like the same examination in depth. Belief as to the person of Christ was determined by the Christian experience of salvation, as may be seen in the Epistle to the Hebrews where the author finds it natural to introduce his treatment of Christ's atoning work with an argument to the effect that he was both human and divine. Similarly, according to Irenaeus:

Unless man had overcome the enemy of man, the enemy would not have been justly vanquished. And again, unless it had been God who had freely given salvation, we could never have possessed it securely. And unless man had been joined to God, he could never have become a partaker of incorruptibility. For it was incumbent upon the Mediator between God and man, by his relationship to both, to bring both to friendship and concord, and present man to God, while he revealed God to man.

The experience of salvation thus leads to the belief that the mediator must have been both God and man.

This simple statement was however insufficient to allay the intellectual curiosity of the Eastern Christians; they wanted to know further, in what sense Jesus was divine and in what sense he was human. The Arian controversy, as reviewed above, provided an answer to the first of these questions with the Nicene affirmation that Christ, being of one substance with the Father, was completely divine. The Apollinarian controversy was the occasion for propounding a reply to the second.

Apollinaris of Laodicea († c. 390) was as concerned as any of his contemporaries to safeguard the reality of salvation, and he was convinced that if the divine were separated from the human in Christ redemption was an impossibility. He therefore—and in this he was representative of the Alexandrian Christology as a whole—approached the question of Christ's humanity from the unity of his person, in order to preserve which he asserted that the Son of God had united himself with human flesh. Since to him the admission of two complete natures would involve a divided personality, he taught that the Word became flesh without assuming a human mind or spirit. This did not mean that the flesh was just an article of clothing which the Word had put on, since it was joined in absolute oneness to the Godhead and had no independent existence apart from it. The Word was indeed the life of the God-man, being the source of his vital energy not only on the spiritual but even on the physical and biological levels. Apollinaris' opponents, and in particular those influenced by the Antiochene school which stressed the reality of the two natures, believed that despite his sincere intentions this teaching undermined the fact of redemption, for it omitted from Christ's humanity the very element that was the seat of sin and most in need of salvation. Accordingly he was condemned at the Council of Constantinople in 381 and the chief ground for rejecting his belief is conveniently summarized by Gregory of Nazianzus:

If anyone has trusted in a man without a mind, he is indeed out of his mind and not worthy to be completely saved. For that which is unassumed is unhealed; but that which has been united to God, this also is saved. . . . Let them not begrudge us a complete salvation, nor equip the Saviour with only the bones and portraiture of a man.

So as a consequence of the debate occasioned by Apollinaris' teaching, the Word-flesh Christology, which many, including Athanasius, had held before him, was discarded in favour of a Word-man Christology: Christ is completely divine and completely human—but this only served to make more acute the problem of the unity of his person. How, once Apollinaris' thesis was rejected, were Christians to conceive of the relationship between the manhood and the Godhead? It will be noted that just as with the Trinitarian question, so here with the Christological problem, the point at issue was that of multiplicity in unity to which philosophical discussions were immediately germane. Of numerous contemporary definitions, some were clearly useless, e.g. the Aristotelian union of mixture according to which two elements could combine to form a third other than its constituents. Two kinds of union however were recognized which found favour with different theologians. First, there is the union of composition or juxtaposition, the resultant being an aggregate of its component parts, and examples, provided by Aristotle, are 'a faggot held together by a band and pieces of wood held together by glue'. Second, there is the union of predominance, of which there was an Aristotelian definition differing from the Stoic. According to Aristotle the resultant of a union of predominance is one of the original constituents, namely the one of the greater power of action; the lesser part does not completely disappear but only remains as a qualitative or quantitative accident of the other. So 'a drop of wine is not mixed with ten thousand gallons of water for the form of the wine is dissolved and changes into the whole of the water'. The wine does not therefore completely disappear but all that remains is its volume or bulk as a quantitative accident. According to the Stoics the resultant of a union of predominance is a mutual coextension, even if there is considerable disparity between the combining elements. 'There is nothing to hinder a drop of wine being mixed with the whole sea,' they said, 'thus a drop will by mixture extend through the whole world.'

In seeking to define the unity of Christ's person, the Nestorians adopted the union of composition, the Eutychians the Aristotelian union of predominance, while the orthodox position was more nearly that of the Stoics.

Whether or not Nestorius himself, who became bishop of Constantinople in 428, was guilty of Nestorianism is much debated, but since what is important for the development of Christological thinking is not what he actually taught but what his opponents understood him to be teaching, it is to this latter that attention must be directed. The Alexandrians, led by Cyril, believed that Nestorius was propounding the thesis that there are two Sons, the Son of God and the Son of man, linked by a purely moral union; so the Incarnate Lord was being split into two distinct persons whose only unity was that of juxtaposition, the Godhead and the manhood existing side by side in a kind of partnership. Christ was thus an ordinary man joined to the Word by harmony of will and the divine favour; this was no incarnation and indeed redemption was undermined since the sufferings of Christ, on this theory, could not be those of God incarnate but those of a mere man.

Nestorius was condemned at the Council of Ephesus in 431 and a reaction against his dualism immediately set in being focused in the teaching of Eutyches († c. 453), archimandrite of a monastery near Constantinople. Of the Alexandrian school and violently anti-Nestorian, he moved to the opposite extreme and, on the basis of the Aristotelian union of predominance, proclaimed that in Christ there was only one nature, the humanity having been absorbed by the divinity, as a drop of wine in ten thousand gallons of water. This theory was in its turn rejected by the Council of Chalcedon, in 451, but before turning to its findings notice should be taken of the orthodox position as it had been maintained in the West and worked out by Cyril of Alexandria († 444) in the East.

It was Tertullian who, as with the doctrine of the Trinity, was the pioneer in Western Christological definition. He taught that the Word of God had become man, but in so doing had not undergone any transformation nor had his manhood lost its essential nature: 'there remain unimpaired the proper being of each substance'. So 'we observe a twofold condition, not confused but conjoined, Jesus in one person at once God and man'. In this statement the three basic factors of Christological orthodoxy are enumerated: 1. The Incarnate Lord is one person. 2. He has two natures. 3. These two natures persist in their entirety unimpaired by the union. Later Western writers did little more than reiterate these fundamental ideas and even Leo the Great († 461), whose 'Tome', an extended epistle devoted to Christology, was accepted as authoritative at Chalcedon, was mainly concerned to codify the beliefs of his predecessors and therefore to assert that while confessing the one Christ, the difference of the natures must be recognized. Leo's teaching however postdates that of Cyril whose letters to Nestorius were also received at Chalcedon.

In Cyril's thinking the point of departure was the pre-existence of the Word. At the incarnation he did not cease to be what he was, but added to it by taking human nature; so both before and after the incarnation he was the same person, the difference being that now he had two natures. There was thus no division because the human nature was his own and had no separate existance apart from him. This in fact was the Stoic union of predominance as is evident from his analogy of the live coal in Isaiah's vision—the charcoal being interpenetrated at all points by the fire while each retains its distinct identity.

The positive beliefs of the Alexandrian school, with its emphasis upon unity, of the Antiochene school, with its emphasis upon the reality of the two natures, and of the Western theologians who held these elements in balance, were summed up in the Definition of Faith promulgated by the Council of Chalcedon, of which the most important section reads as follows:

Following, then, the holy Fathers, we all unanimously teach that our Lord Jesus Christ is to us one and the same Son, the same perfect in Godhead, the same perfect in manhood; truly God and truly man; the same (consisting) of a rational soul and a body; of the same substance as the Father as to his Godhead, and the same of one substance with us as to his manhood: like us in all things, except for sin; begotten of the Father before ages as to his Godhead, and in the last days, the same, for us and for our salvation, of Mary Theotokos as to his manhood; one and the same Christ, Son, Lord, only-begotten, made known in two natures (which exist) without confusion, without change, without division, without separation; the difference of the natures being in no way taken away because of the union, but rather the properties of each nature being preserved, and (both) concurring into one person and one hypostasis—not parted or divided into two persons, but one and the same Son and only-begotten, the divine Word, the Lord Jesus Christ.

So the unity of Christ's person was affirmed and the principle of 'recognizing' the natures was established. The Godhead and the manhood are two, though only in contemplation. In the one person are shown forth and are therefore to be recognized both natures, which nevertheless concur into one person.

Unfortunately the findings of the Council were not universally accepted because of a misunderstanding of the terminology employed by the framers of the Definition. Certain representatives of the Alexandrian school interpreted the word 'nature' to mean 'person'. When therefore it was stated that Christ was 'made known in two "natures"', they believed this to be Nestorianism all over again, involving the belief that Christ was 'made known in two "persons"'. These Monophysites, as they were called, therefore went into opposition and further debate took place leading to a greater clarification of belief and culminating in the teaching of Leontius of Byzantium († c. 543).

Leontius' beliefs did not differ essentially from those of Cyril but he gave them more succinct expression and made use of a more exact terminology. Cyril, in opposing Nestorianism, had declared that the humanity of Christ was not 'a man'; it was rather impersonal. Leontius' main contribution was in affirming that it was inpersonal. The 'person' of Jesus Christ was the pre-existent Son of God who, at his incarnation, united to himself not another person but human nature which was his own —the human personality was thus that of the divine subject under submission to physical conditions. Here again human analogies tend to break down, as they do in relation to the doctrine of the Trinity, since Christ himself was unique. Moreover it is customary to think of union in terms of the coming together of two entities, previously existing separately; but the humanity of Christ had no separate existence, no existence at all, before the incarnation; the only pre-existing entity was the Son of God who assumed human nature which thereupon became personal in him since it was his humanity. This teaching was endorsed by the fifth ecumenical council of Constantinople in 553, and was reaffirmed by John of Damascus in his *De Fide Orthodoxa*: 'He took on himself the first-fruits of our flesh, and these not as having a separate existence, or as being formerly an individual and thus assumed by him, but as existing in his own person. For the person of the divine Word itself became the person of the flesh.'

This belief, that in Christ there are two natures, had as its corollaries the idea that he had two operations, divine and human, and two wills. These conclusions were however not drawn until the opposite had been argued in the Monergist, i.e. one operation, and Monethelite, i.e. one will, controversies. So at the sixth ecumenical council at Constantinople in 680–1 it was laid down that in Jesus Christ there are 'two natural wills and two natural operations without division, without change, without separation, without confusion, according to the teaching of the holy Fathers. And these two natural wills are not contrary the one to the other. . . . But his human will follows, and that not as resisting or reluctant, but rather as subject to his divine and omnipotent will.'

This involved no split personality, since, as John of Damascus pointed out, 'we hold that it is one and the same person who wills and operates naturally in both natures, out of which and in which and also which is Christ our Lord', for 'his human will clearly follows his divine will and wills that which the divine will willeth it to will'. Hence there is one theandric operation of redemption, the two natures with their wills and operations concurring into the one person of the God-man. Thus Christological belief achieved its classic expression to which the mediaeval divines had little or nothing to add.

Repeated emphasis has so far been laid upon the extent to which Christian belief was the outcome of Christian experience. It was because they knew they were saved through Christ that the doctrine of the Trinity and Christology assumed such importance. But this experience involved a present relationship with their Lord which they were convinced not even death could interrupt; sharing already by anticipation in Christ's risen life, they awaited the consummation of God's plan for the world in confident faith and expressed this certainty in the doctrine of the resurrection.

Of the apostolic writers Paul is the only one who considers the subject in any detail. Holding, as any other Jew, that man is an ensouled body, he believed in the embodied nature of the resurrection-life and, rejecting any crude notion of physical re-animation, he understood this to involve transformation or transfiguration. Thus by the resurrection of the body he meant not the reassembling of certain material particles but the raising to newness of life of the whole organic personality. In I Corinthians 15 he expounded this by the analogy of a seed which is planted in the ground and, ceasing to be a seed, grows into a plant. The two, seed and plant, are in a sense identical but between them there is the critical point when the seed dies and is transformed into the growing plant—there is a persisting subject with a change of predicate. The connexion between them is the sovereign power of God who 'gives it a body, even as it pleases him'. So the body of the believer is changed from flesh, which by its nature decays, into glory, yet the personality by no means disappears: 'it is sown a mortal body; it is raised a spiritual body'.

The later history of this belief represents a turning away from this Pauline conception under the influence of the accounts of the Resurrection of Christ. Failing to appreciate that the form these took was essential to convince the apostles that their Master was no mere ghost, as they were ready to suppose, but the conqueror of death, many Christians understood them, not as a unique series of events accommodated to the sense perceptions of Jesus' followers but as a revelation of the nature of the final resurrection. Thus, contrary to Paul, they asserted the resurrection of the flesh and while many regarded this as involving transformation, the popular view, that tended more and more to prevail, was that of physical re-animation, defended on the somewhat specious grounds that with God all things are possible. Nevertheless it was this belief that sustained the courage of many a Christian in the dark days of the break-up of the Roman empire, for the pressure of contemporary circumstances tends to direct attention to certain beliefs rather than to others. When the present life seems vain and the future alone holds out any hope, it is easy to turn from salvation as an immediate experience to the vision of the resurrection and the last judgement as bringing freedom from unrelenting toil and misery. Small wonder that as the Middle Ages were ushered in amidst political anarchy and economic chaos the futuristic element in the Christian faith should assume more and more importance, and yet in the Creeds there was preserved a statement of the full range of Christian belief to provide a continual counterbalance to partial or over-emphases.

In the Apostolic Age there existed no creed in the sense of an official and textually determined formula, although there was quite evidently a recurring pattern of belief. Hence Paul refers to 'the faith that was once for all delivered unto the saints', and to 'that form of teaching whereunto ye were delivered'. The tasks of preaching the Gospel, of preparing candidates for baptism, of requiring a confession of faith at baptism, together with the rites of exorcism and the liturgy itself, all these were factors which worked on the recognized body of teaching to crystallize into conventional summaries. These summaries assumed one of two forms, declaratory and interrogatory. The second of these grew out of the questions put to baptismal candidates and was triadic since the framework was the Matthean command to baptize in the threefold Name. The declaratory type consisted originally of one, two or three members, depending upon whether the statement of belief was in Jesus, in the Father and the Son or in the three persons of the Trinity. Its content was eventually enlarged under the influence of the regular instruction given to catechumens. It was indeed the increasing influx of converts that necessitated careful organization on the part of the Church to prevent its being swamped by large numbers of folk with false notions of the content and meaning of Christianity.

The stereotyped confessions produced to meet this need were associated with special ceremonies to enhance their importance. These were the *traditio* or handing-over when the candidates were told the creed, and the *redditio* or handing-back when they recited it to the bishop after memorizing it. So the original positive function of creeds was to set forth Christian beliefs—any anti-heretical purpose was secondary in the period prior to Nicaea—and this is brought out well by Cyril of Jerusalem in an address which probably accompanied the *traditio*:

In learning the Faith and professing it, acquire and keep that only which is now delivered to you by the Church, and which has been built up strongly out of all the Scriptures. For since all cannot read the Scriptures, some because they are illiterate and some because they have not the leisure, in order that the soul might not perish through ignorance, we comprise the whole doctrine of the Faith in a few lines. This summary I wish you both to commit to memory when I recite it and to rehearse it carefully among yourselves, not writing it upon paper but engraving it by memory on your hearts. . . . I wish you also to keep this as a provision through the whole course of your life, and beside this to receive no other, neither if we ourselves should change and contradict our present teaching, nor if any adverse angel, disguised as an angel of light, should wish to lead you astray. So for the present simply listen while I say the Creed, and commit it to memory; but at the proper season expect the confirmation out of Holy Scripture of each part of its contents. For the articles of the faith were not composed as it seemed good to men, but the most important points are collected out of all the Scriptures to make up one comprehensive summary of the Faith. And just as the mustard seed in one small grain contains many branches, so also this Creed has embraced in a few words all the knowledge of godliness in the Old and New Testaments.

Typical of these pre-baptismal declarations of belief is that known as the Apostles' Creed. This was originally a local creed developed at Rome, which may be traced back to at least the early third century, but only assumed its present form much later in the sixth and seventh centuries probably in south-west France. Side by side with such local products, there were also from the fourth century conciliar creeds, beginning with the creed of the Council of Nicaea, deliberately anti-Arian in its intention, and leading up to the creed of Constantinople, 381, which is the one usually referred to today as the 'Nicene' Creed. Of all existing creeds this is the only one that has received universal approval and so may be quoted in its original form as a convenient summary of the beliefs of the Church:

We believe

In one God the Father almighty, maker of heaven and earth, of all things visible and invisible;

And in one Lord Jesus Christ, the only-begotten Son of God, begotten from the Father before all ages, light from light, true God from true God, begotten not made, of one substance with the Father, through whom all things were made; who for us men and for our salvation came down from heaven, and was incarnate from the Holy Spirit and the Virgin Mary, and was made man, and was crucified for us under Pontius Pilate, and suffered and was buried, and rose again the third day according to the Scriptures, and ascended into heaven, and sits at the right hand of the Father, and will come again with glory to judge living and dead, of whose kingdom there will be no end;

And in the Holy Spirit, the Lord and life-giver, who proceeds from the Father, who with the Father and the Son is co-worshipped and co-glorified, who spoke through the prophets; and in one holy Catholic and apostolic Church. We confess one Baptism for the remission of sins; we look forward to the resurrection of the dead and the life of the world to come.

Amen.

Epilogue

On the morning of Christmas Day in the year 800, Charles, king of the Franks, entered the Vatican basilica in Rome and, as he rose from his devotions immediately before the beginning of the mass, the pope, Leo III, advanced towards him, placed a crown upon his head and knelt in obeisance, to the accompaniment of a prolonged acclamation: 'Life and victory to Charles, the most pious Augustus, crowned by God, great and peaceful emperor of the Romans.' This restoration of the ancient empire of the West marks yet another stage in the history of the Church and raises, at the same time, in an acute form the question: at what date does the history of the early Church become the history of the Church in the Middle Ages?

To this query no certain answer can be given. It is indeed the practice of historians to divide their subject into periods, to mark the inception of the modern era, for example, by the year of Columbus' voyage across the Atlantic, but convenient though this may be, it is doubtful if anyone imagines that it corresponds to any reality. History is a continuing process, and if there be any truth in the dictum that the child is father to the man, it is equally true of the ages of Church history. Already in the fifth century many of the features that are regarded as characteristic of the Middle Ages are making themselves visible, already in the teaching of Augustine the mediaeval divines had found their master. It is true that after the first half-millenium of its existence the Church had a structure, an inner life, a social concern and a system of beliefs whereby it

had achieved self-consciousness and was readily identifiable—
in this sense these centuries witnessed the making of the
Church.

But if the Church is true to its nature and remains conscious of its mission, it can never be just a static monolith, it
must be continually in the making. This is a story that has no
end and even the vision of a reunited Christendom, which in-
spires so many today, will, if realized, seem to future generations but another episode in a continuing life which only has
its consummation, according to the belief of its members, in
eternity. Yet if 'in my beginning is my end', it is to the early
days of the Church that we must turn to understand what it is
today, and, more particularly, since the Church exists to bear
witness to certain historical events upon which it is founded, a
knowledge of the classical interpretation of those events and of
its living out in terms of human history at a time more proxi-
mate to them than our own becomes a matter of contemporary
concern. Yet these events were eschatological events, since
they marked the inbreaking of the 'End'; hence 'in my end is
my beginning' also applies to the Church. So the Church has
a twofold aspect—at once rigid and fixed, for its being rests
on the unchangeable events of the past, and dynamic and
changing, for it rests also, so its members believe, upon the
continuing activity of the Holy Spirit stretching forward into
the future. Time and eternity, static and dynamic, God and
man—these are paradoxes essential to it as its formation
continues.

Books for Further Reading

For the missionary endeavour, the reader should consult A. Harnack, *The Expansion of Christianity in the First Three Centuries*, I and II (1905), and the first volume of K. S. Latourette, *A History of the Expansion of Christianity* (1947). On the structure of the Church Edward Schillebeeckx's *Ministry* (1981) gives a judicious account of one aspect. The early history of the parochial system has been investigated by G. W. O. Addleshaw, *The Beginnings of the Parochial System* (1953). A brief introduction to canon law may be found in *The Canon Law of the Church of England* (1947). Two excellent studies of the relations of Church and State and of the early schisms are by S. L. Greenslade, *Church and State from Constantine to Theodosius* (1954) and *Schism in the Early Church* (1953), while for the persecutions see W. H. C. Frend, *Martyrdom and Persecution in the Early Church* (1965). On the social history of the Church consult J. G. Davies, *Daily Life in the Early Church* (1952) and *Social Life of Early Christians* (1954). A useful introduction to the practice of prayer is to be found in F. G. Jay, *Origen's Treatise on Prayer* (1954), while Bible reading is examined by A. Harnack, *Bible Reading in the Early Church* (1912). For monks see Derwas Chitty, *The Desert a City* (1966) and the preface by O. Chadwick, to his *Western Asceticism* (1958). The history of the eucharist is still most readably set out by G. Dix, *The Shape of the Liturgy*, although first published as long ago as 1945. For the calendar there is A. A. McArthur, *The Evolution of the Christian Year* (1953). The architectural setting of worship is described by R. Krautheimer, *Early Christian and Byzantine Architecture* (1965). Finally for the development of Christian beliefs see two works, which have gone through numerous editions, by J. N. D. Kelly, *Early Christian Creeds* (1950) and *Early Christian Doctrines* (1958).

Index